W9-BIC-027

ZONE
TO
WIN

ORGANIZING
TO COMPETE
IN AN AGE OF
DISRUPTION

GEOFFREY A. MOORE

DIVERSIONBOOKS

Diversion Books
A Division of Diversion Publishing Corp.
443 Park Avenue South, Suite 1008
New York, New York 10016
www.DiversionBooks.com

For more information, email info@diversionbooks.com

First Diversion Books edition November 2015.
Print ISBN: 978-1-68230-171-5
eBook ISBN: 978-1-68230-170-8

To Noah Oak and the next generation

Contents

Foreword

In 2013, Geoff was drafting the third edition of his classic book *Crossing the Chasm*, and he asked me about using Salesforce to illustrate some of his management principles. Many of the companies cited in the first and second editions of the book were no longer around. I was excited that Salesforce would be part of the updated book, but I also shared with Geoff that we were struggling to stay agile and focused as we grew very fast and expanded our portfolio of products. Salesforce was the leading customer relationship management platform, but internally we had developed too many conflicts and were getting pulled in too many directions. We were growing fast and innovating at a rapid pace, but we didn't have a handle on how to organize ourselves in ways that optimized for both established business units and new investment areas.

Geoff agreed to interview key managers on our teams to diagnose what was causing our dysfunction and suggest solutions. During the process, he came up with the concept of *zone management.* It's a deceptively simple and powerful model for resolving conflicts and accelerating business transformation.

Zone management is about dividing and conquering, establishing independent zones, each with what at Salesforce we call a V2MOM—Vision, Values, Methods, Obstacles, and Measures. Disruptive innovation—incubating or scaling new products or business opportunities—must be segregated from sustaining innovation—making improvements to existing entities. And, revenue performance—financial commitments from the more established parts of the business—must be separated from enabling investments—funding and resourcing new product and businesses opportunities. The zones act in parallel and interoperate with each other, but not in lockstep.

By looking at Salesforce through the lens of zone management, Geoff helped us improve our ability to execute in many phases of our business. Following our engagement, Geoff continued to flesh out the zone management concept, working with leaders at Microsoft to add the perspective of a forty-year-old company that was dealing with far more complexity. The end result is *Zone to Win: Organizing to Compete in an Age of Disruption.*

For any company, regardless of size or industry, *Zone to Win* is the playbook for building enterprises that reach escape velocity—orienting to the future and avoiding the inertial pull of the past. It's the playbook for not just surviving but succeeding in today's disruptive, connected, fast-paced business world.

Marc Benioff, Chairman and CEO, Salesforce
August 2015

Preface

Zone to Win is the seventh, and with any luck the last, in a sequence of books about the impact of disruptive technology on business strategy and company valuations. The series began with *Crossing the Chasm*, first published in 1990. That book addressed the market development challenges venture-backed startups face when trying to grow beyond an early-adopter customer base and win mainstream customers. Its lessons have stood the test of time, with more than a million copies sold worldwide and a third edition with all new case examples released in 2014.

In 1995 *Crossing the Chasm* was followed by *Inside the Tornado*, which focused on the winner-take-all competitions that unfold when disruptive technologies are mature enough to displace their incumbent predecessors. It in turn was followed by *The Gorilla Game*, coauthored with Tom Kippola and Paul Johnson in 1998, which focused on the implications of tornado dynamics for company valuations that were at the time eye-popping, to say the least. This was the era of the dot-com bubble, or as my colleague Paul Wiefels likes to call it, the Time of the Great Happiness. It all ended in 2001.

With the bursting of the dot-com bubble, the focus of my consulting shifted to established enterprises (the ones left standing!) and how they might expect to engage with these same market dynamics. This led to a shift in perspective from that of the disruptor to that of the disruptee. It also led to a second sequence of three books, each presenting a set of frameworks to help guide management through challenging times. They included the Core/Context framework from *Living on the Fault Line*, the Return on Innovation framework from *Dealing with Darwin*, and the Hierarchy of Powers framework from *Escape Velocity*. All three describe strategies to better engage with disruptive innovation. What they did not do, on the other hand, was solve for problems of organization and execution.

That is the role of this book. It has been made possible through lessons learned from two consulting relationships, one with Salesforce and the other with Microsoft. Each brought me into contact with an exceptional leader and a team of executives intent not only on doing the right things but also on doing things right. Like everything in the tech sector, this too is a work in progress, but enough has been proven that it is now time to share the results.

What follows is a highly prescriptive approach—indeed, a playbook—for organizing and managing established enterprises of any size in a time of category disruption. It is based on dividing up enterprise activity into four zones and managing each zone independently from the other three. In so doing it is designed to address two challenges. The first is to help management teams in established franchises manage the resource allocation challenges of onboarding a new line of business while maintaining commitments to the existing ones. This we call playing *zone offense*. The second is to help these same teams organize themselves to beat back a disruptive innovator's attack targeting one of their mature core businesses. We call this playing *zone defense*. Taken together they constitute *zone management*, a discipline intended to let enterprises compete at full strength when it comes to engaging with the disruptive innovations that are reshaping so much of our world.

CHAPTER ONE
A Crisis of Prioritization

What makes modern business different? Simply put, speed plus disruption. Wave after wave of next-generation technology is continually transforming the landscape of business, both inside the tech sector, where the new offers are germinated, and everywhere else outside it, where they are largely consumed. This results in two imperatives for any established enterprise. In markets where you want to be the disruptor, where you want to play offense, you must *catch the next wave*. At the same time, in those markets where your current franchise is the incumbent and is itself under a disruptive attack, you have to play defense in order to *prevent the next wave from catching you*.

Either way, you are about to experience a crisis of prioritization, one that has stumped all but the very best of our top companies.

Catching the Next Wave

If you are in high tech, or for that matter in any other sector characterized by recurrent disruption, you can't sit still. You simply have to be a growth company. If your enterprise is not in a growth category, if all you are doing is optimizing your current market positions, you are a sitting duck. Operationally, that means that at any given point in time you must find a way to participate meaningfully in one or more emerging high-growth categories. You need to find a rising tide to float your boat. You need to catch the next wave to propel you forward.

Rapid category growth is directly linked to disruptive innovation because it only occurs at the front end of a new adoption life cycle. That is, when an emerging technology reaches its tipping point, when it goes inside the tornado— be that in digital marketing, electric cars, cloud computing, or the like—the market, heretofore having been playing a wait-and-see game, now rushes to take it up. This results in a massive wave of net new spending, initiating a *secular* expansion with growth rates typically well north of 20 percent for a period of typically five to seven years. Such secular shifts in spending are one-time affairs. That means you either catch these waves when they crest or wait around for the next one.

To be sure, growth does not stop once the secular surge subsides, but it does moderate. From here on out for the life of the category, growth will be a function of *cyclical*, not secular, forces—tracking primarily to overall growth in the GDP, modulated by new product introductions and expansion into new market segments. As the category continues to mature, ecosystems will consolidate around the market leaders that will in turn get the lion's share of future returns. Thus, category power gets converted into company power. This is how Fortune 500 franchises are made. All these dynamics are captured in stock price and market valuation. During the secular growth phase, investors price up the stocks of first movers dramatically, often to ten times next year's projected revenues or more. They see the rising tide that floats all boats, and they know that the companies that catch this new wave will substantially outperform those that don't. By contrast, once the category transitions into cyclical growth, valuations will moderate to around one to two times the current revenue, the focus shifting to price-to-earnings ratio instead, a metric that better reflects competitive advantage in a mature category. In this context, valuations for all the companies in the sector become less volatile and begin to oscillate around a mean. As a result, even the best-performing enterprises in mature categories struggle mightily to budge their market caps—not because their deeds are not admirable, but because they have been anticipated and already priced into their stock. Investors who see no reason to expect either risks or returns to be substantially different in the future see no basis for bidding up or down the value of the equity.

What does change stock price dramatically, on the other hand, is entry into an emerging growth category at a meaningful scale. When a company's participation in such a category exceeds, say, 10 percent of its total enterprise revenue, and moreover is on a growth trajectory to reach 15 to 20 percent in the foreseeable future, then investors take out a fresh sheet of paper to evaluate the potential returns from this new earnings engine. At minimum they will add these returns to their established models, but more often, particularly if the synergies look compelling, they will also top things off with an additional price premium.

Consider some examples from the technology sector, the epicenter of category disruptions. At the time of this writing, over the past ten years the Nasdaq has increased 148% in value. During this time the valuation of Oracle increased 229%, EMC 92%, Microsoft 88%, SAP 70%, Cisco 53%, and HP 42%, while IBM's valuation dropped 39%. This is the kind of oscillation around the mean we see in the valuation of established enterprises in mature categories, even when many delivered superior earnings throughout this period. By contrast, in that same period, Apple's valuation increased 2,378%, Salesforce's 1,320%, and Amazon's 1,197%. None of these increases had much to do with their performance in their established mature franchises in, respectively, personal computers, CRM, and e-commerce. Instead, investors were rewarding Apple for catching three new category waves (digital music, smartphones, and tablets), Salesforce for catching two (cloud platform as a service and cloud marketing automation), and Amazon for catching a single whopper (cloud computing as a service).

The key takeaway here from a growth investor's perspective is that when it comes to generating serious upside returns, catching the next wave is all that really matters. This perspective has not been lost on executives and boards of directors in established enterprises. They all have equity-based compensation systems that incentivize them to pursue these opportunities aggressively. They all pay close attention to growth opportunities. They all seek surpluses on their balance sheets and free cash flow from their operating income to invest in emerging categories. They all employ super-smart strategy experts to analyze their current portfolios of businesses, to assess their landscape of opportunities, and to identify the best ones to target. They all have annual plans that set aside considerable resources to pursue these targets both organically and through acquisitions. The CEO and the board are completely aligned in the understanding that this is their highest overall long-term priority. What could possibly go wrong?

Well, perhaps we should ask the CEOs of any of the following companies that question:

COMPANIES THAT MISSED THE NEXT WAVE

Burroughs - Sperry Univac - Honeywell
Control Data - MSA - McCormack & Dodge
Cullinet - Cincom - ADR - CA - DEC
Data General - Wang - Prime - Tandem
Daisy - Calma - Valid - Apollo - Silicon Graphics
Sun - Atari - Osborne - Commodore - Casio
Palm - Sega - WordPerfect - Lotus - Ashton Tate
Borland - Informix - Ingres - Sybase - BEA
Seibel - PowerSoft - Nortel - Lucent - 3Com
Banyan - Novell - Pacific Bell - Qwest -
America West - Nynex - Bell South - Netscape
MySpace - Inktomi - Ask Jeeves - AOL
Blackberry - Motorola - Nokia - Sony

I have spent the entirety of my business career working in the technology sector, and I can assure you, if you are looking for next waves to catch, there is no better place to hang out. Nevertheless, there are fifty-six companies on this list of companies that failed to do so. Look at the names. These were not the losers; these were the winners! These were not our worst management teams; these were our best! And yet every single one of them missed every single one of their efforts to catch the next big wave—hundreds and hundreds of misses with nary a single hit. Why is this so hard?

It turns out, to disrupt someone else's business, you have to add a net new line of business to your own portfolio. This is, in effect, a form of elective surgery, one that can be scheduled at will. Because it is voluntary, because we get to choose the time and place of engagement, we are led to believe we have things under control. Unfortunately, nothing could be further from the truth. The real truth is most companies take run after run at this hurdle, but each time, at the critical juncture, that moment when you have to either go big or go home, they shy away. Normally it is not until their own legacy business comes under attack that they can summon the will to change, but by then it is usually too late.

Why? What's going on?

Adding a new line of business to an existing portfolio creates a *crisis of prioritization*. Such efforts are easy to get started, but as momentum begins to build it becomes increasingly clear that there are not going to be enough resources to go around, so how are they going to get allocated? Partially this is a question of quantity—how much of your resources should you continue to deploy into your established lines of business versus how much to divert into the emerging new one? Partially it is a question of quality—how much value should you assign to achieving additional gains from your established lines of business versus new gains from your emerging new one? And partially it is a question of politics and power—how much are you willing to challenge the entrenched interests that demand and reward short-term returns versus how much you are willing to risk on a bet that requires immediate sacrifices in hopes of achieving exceptional long-term gains?

At the core of this crisis of prioritization is a battle for resources in the go-to-market functions—sales, marketing, professional services, and partner development. To add a net new line of business to the portfolio, the enterprise has to stretch its go-to-market capacity dramatically to meet the needs of both its established businesses and its next-generation initiatives. It turns out, however, not only are there not enough resources to go around, there is no efficient way to expand them. Here's why. Marketing, selling, servicing, and partnering in any emerging category are radically inefficient processes, especially when compared to established lines of business. For starters, prospective customers have no budget allocated for the new category of offering—it is simply too new. So you have to work with the line-of-business executives in those companies to show them the possibilities and persuade them to take the risk. This takes time. It also requires relationships your salespeople are not likely to have (theirs are with the other side of the customer house, the side that is perfectly happy with the status quo, the one that has budget already allocated for your offers, and the one that is not likely to be very happy about you engaging elsewhere in their company). This makes developing the market for an emerging category both challenging and risky—you might not succeed in getting budget approved, or you might get budget approved only to lose the deal to a competitor. And to make matters worse, this is not a go-to-market motion your existing team is good at—they are much better suited to selling more of the old stuff via their established relationships.

Now, the standard way to address these problems is to overlay a sales force that does specialize in this sort of market development and is able to focus solely on the new initiative. At the outset, this approach is promising—it actually does work—but as the business begins to scale, it gets more and more expensive to operate. Moreover, as it seeks to engage with more and more of your installed base, your account managers with established customer relationships become increasingly reluctant to bring in the new team because their presence can destabilize a deal in the works or damage a long-standing relationship by going over the head of your traditional buyer. Because of this kind of inherent friction, scaling a single disruptive innovation can easily absorb 10 percent or more of your total go-to-market envelope before adoption reaches the tipping point.

And that raises a host of other problems. Increased expense with less revenue means your profit margins will take a hit. This can deflate your stock price and alienate your investor base, potentially to the extent that it could put your company in play. Meanwhile, your current ecosystem of partners is getting restless. They make their living supporting your established lines of business and are feeling threatened by this new disruptive innovation. And inside your own company the leaders of your established lines of business are feeling increasingly squeezed themselves and are signaling that they cannot make their numbers without getting a bigger share of the go-to-market pie. Of course they can spare a modest amount of their go-to-market resources, but *10 percent?*

The net result of all this is painful but clear. It is just barely possible that an established enterprise, through intense commitment, clear prioritization, and laser focus, can grow a single net new line of business to scale while still maintaining its commitment to its existing franchises. That said, it is absolute lunacy to think it can do two or more at the same time. Unfortunately, that is precisely what the standard playbook for strategic portfolio management calls for you to do—*don't put all your eggs in one basket!* That may sound like good advice until you realize it brought all fifty-six of the companies we listed to their knees.

When a go-to-market organization is charged to scale two or more new franchises while at the same time being expected to make the numbers in the established lines of business, anyone with experience knows this is simply not going to happen. This triggers a cascade of passive-aggressive behaviors in which the new lines of business are given lots of showcase attention, but everyone who wants to make quota focuses the bulk of their time on the tried and true. Sooner or later the sponsors of the new category have no choice but to fold their tents, allowing the "wiser" sort to give each other I-told-you-so looks. It is hard to imagine a more useless waste of human capital.

So, first things first: When it comes to making a big bet on your next big thing, pick *one*. Not two, not three—one. This is the single most important job a CEO has. Choose one thing to be your enterprise's next big thing, and then deliver on that future—to customers, to shareholders, to partners, to employees, and to your industry as a whole. If someone questions you putting all your eggs in one basket, just tell them, "In our company we like to lay eggs one at a time. By the way, we find most chickens do too."

If your company could catch a new wave just once in a decade, it would be world-class. IBM did. Digital Equipment Corporation did not. Microsoft did. Lotus and Novell did not. That said, as we already noted, Steve Jobs did it three times in one decade. What is the single most important lesson executive teams can learn from his performance? All of Apple's new lines of business were brought to scale *one at a time!* Steve was a challenging person to work with, but there was never any question as to what his priorities were. His core principle was: "We have one team working on one thing." He might whiff—the Lisa comes to mind here—but he would not waffle.

Fifty-six other CEOs played their hands differently. In effect, they did waffle. They were torn between funding the current business and backing the next big thing, and they did not want to put all their eggs in one basket. So they peanut-buttered their resource allocations, making sure every credible disruptive innovation got its fair share of support, but always with a tilt toward making the number on the back of the established lines of business. That by default is a kind of prioritization in its own right, but it is a painfully wasteful one, since it absolutely guarantees you will never catch the next wave, even as you spend all your scarce discretionary resources under the pretense that you can.

This brings us to the heart of the crisis of prioritization: At the core you must deliver on two conflicting objectives. On the one hand, you must maintain your established franchises for the life of their respective business models, adjusting to declining revenue growth by optimizing for increasing earnings growth. This objective most of the fifty-six CEOs did indeed deliver on. At the same time, every decade or so you must get your company into one net new line of business that has exceptionally high revenue growth. This they did not.

To stay relevant in any sector characterized by frequent disruptive innovations, you have to do both. That's the problem facing every CEO in high tech. That's why high tech needs a new playbook. But what about everybody else?

Coping with the Next Wave

Unless you are Rip Van Winkle, you are now well aware that waves of disruptive innovation are no longer confined just to high tech. They have now been unleashed on whole swaths of the world's economy. In media, in advertising, in travel and hospitality, in retail, in automotive, and in transportation, companies like Netflix, Google, Airbnb, Amazon, Tesla, and Uber have put companies like CBS, Omnicom, Hilton, Walmart, General Motors, and Hertz back on their heels.

And this is only just the beginning. What industry can possibly be exempt from massive reengineering now that every person on the planet is carrying the equivalent of a 1990 supercomputer in his or her pocket or purse? What legacy business process can possibly remain intact given the digitization of all information and universal availability of wireless communication? Even if disruption has not touched your sector directly as yet, how can you possibly imagine that your company will not get caught up in one or more of these maelstroms sooner or later—and more likely than not, sooner?

This is not about you catching the next wave. This is about the next wave catching you. In situations like this, you aren't playing offense. You are playing defense. This too will create a crisis of prioritization, albeit one that will appear to unfold in slow motion. Take Kodak, for example. It hired George Fisher out of Motorola in 1993 to deal with the disruption of digital photography. It went bankrupt almost twenty years later because of that disruption. There was not one of those years when management and the board ignored this problem. But still they could not solve it. Why should things be different for you?

Well, first of all, not every disruption is of the Kodak variety. When the next wave catches you, its disruptive impact can be felt at different levels in your enterprise depending on how close to your core business it lands. The question you want to answer at the outset, therefore, is whether you are being disrupted at the level of your infrastructure model, your operating model, or your business model.

Take the disruptive impact of mobile smartphones as an example. If you are in the real estate business, smartphones don't actually disrupt your business model or even your operating model to any great extent. You are still going to make your living earning a commission on real estate sales, and you are still going to operate as a network of agents. That means you can absorb the disruption of smartphones at the *infrastructure model* level, incorporating them into your marketing and communication systems, improving both the agent's productivity and the customer's service experience without changing anything more material. This is something like buying a new car. Yes, it will take some investment, and yes, it will take some getting used to as well, but the changes are reasonably straightforward to manage, and it is not an earth-shaking event.

Suppose, however, you are in the airline business, and you are competing for high-margin business travelers. These are people who live on their smartphones. They want to use them to book flights, secure their boarding passes, get flight statuses, check frequent flyer points, and the like. If you don't offer them a powerful modern mobile app, they are going to take their business elsewhere. This means you have to change your *operating model*. Yes, you need new infrastructure, but it goes way beyond that. Over time you will redirect your investments in personnel and equipment for travel agents, check-in counters and kiosks, lounge services, in-flight services, boarding processes, and the like, all to adapt them to the new mobile landscape. This is much more disruptive than simply swapping out infrastructure. There are major process changes that must be accompanied by and coordinated with your infrastructure modernization. Whole budgets and job descriptions will get rewritten or even eliminated. Not only is this going to be expensive to undertake but also the ROI will not come until the out years, making a highly unattractive dent in the current year's performance, not to mention the performance-based compensation of the executive team.

You are not just buying a new car here; it is more like you are moving to a new city and undertaking a new commute. For sure, this will generate enough inertial resistance to create a *challenge* of prioritization, but not, I would argue, a *crisis*. That's because, when you step back and take the long view, the changes required are not truly life-threatening. You typically have a reasonable amount of time to manage them provided you hop to it, and overall you can be fairly optimistic about getting through an operating model disruption, perhaps after a couple of dodgy years.

But now let us suppose you are in the advertising business. You are best known for your creative ads, but you make the bulk of your revenues placing those ads in media buys, be that with TV, radio, print media, or billboards. Media consumption, however, has shifted dramatically to online digital properties, initially to desktops and laptops, now increasingly to tablets and even more so to smartphones. Here media buying has been completely disrupted by the likes of Google, Yahoo!, Appnexus, and their ilk, not to mention newer players like RocketFuel and AudienceScience—it's all done by computer algorithms. All your buying expertise, your whole network of ecosystem relationships, has been rendered irrelevant. Not only can you not charge a premium for placing ads, you're not really in a position to perform the task at all. Sure, you can still charge for creative, but that is a time-and-materials business model that has nothing like the scalability of your traditional commission model. Of course, you can still charge for "old media" in the old ways, but the tide is going out on this book of business, and you are going to have to replace it with something. In short, you have no option but to change your *business model.* This isn't about buying a new car or even moving to a new town and learning a new commute. This about getting fired and having to find a whole new job!

Business model disruptions are where all the train wrecks happen. They are the "Kodak moments" that the press is compelled to write about and that executives in other companies read with such schadenfreude. They are the ultimate consequence of the next wave catching you. People say, when this happens, that you should have learned to disrupt yourself. You should have realized that if somebody is going to eat your lunch, it might as well be you. Well, in the interests of public safety and managerial sanity, let me share a secret with you: *No established enterprise can reasonably expect to change its core business model, ever.* All that stuff about how you have to learn to disrupt yourself—it's baloney. It can't be done. There is simply too much inertial momentum tied up in your internal systems, your customer relationships, your company culture, your supply chain processes, your ecosystem of partners, and your investors' expectations. By the time you dismantled all of these, there would be nothing left for you to repurpose. All you would have done is chased away the remainder of the business that was yours to have.

So what must you do instead to prevent the next wave from catching you? Two things, actually. First, on an emergency basis, you must race to modernize your existing operating model as best you can, incorporating enough of the next-generation technology to at least blunt the impact of the disruptor in the short term. Thus, for example, all the major advertising agencies have developed digital ad-buying desks to offer as an in-house service. This buys you time by helping maintain and even extend the inertial momentum of your existing business relationships. It is not, however, a permanent fix, as you are competing on the other guy's turf, and he plays the game much better than you do. So second, in parallel, you must turn to your own portfolio of next-generation opportunities to accelerate your own progress toward catching some other wave of disruption emerging in some other category. In the case of advertising, it turns out that digital marketing is a tough nut to crack. There is a lot of creative energy concentrated inside these agencies to apply to this problem and a lot of trapped value out in the world that would pay back the effort to do so. The challenge is to find new ways to express and monetize their talent. Hard as this may be to execute, it is the only thing that can provide the growth burst needed to get back in the game. The difference is that here agencies will be disrupting someone else's legacy business model, not their own.

Of course, this begs the question: Why weren't they doing this second step all along—isn't that the whole point of portfolio management? Yes it is, and yes they should have been. But here, let me say, they have a lot of company, and once again the culprit is a crisis of prioritization. The legacy business model in advertising, like the ones in mainframe computing, enterprise software maintenance agreements, OEM licenses for operating systems, inkjet cartridges, automobile dealerships, taxi medallions, luxury retail, patented pharmaceuticals, investment banking, venture capital, and *premier cru* Bordeaux wines, is based on profit margins that have been locked in for a very long time and have subsequently lost correlation with the value received.

Now, from an investor's point of view, this is great: you guys are investing low and selling high—it's like printing money! *Don't stop!* But, of course, stop is precisely what you have to do. Or rather, "transition." You have to get your company off the drug. Unfortunately, in the short term you have no incentive to do so, and every incentive not to. As we have already discussed, your mature franchise is valued very differently from growth ones. For you the market focuses on your P/E ratio (price to earnings) rather than your P/S ratio (price to sales). As long as those earnings keep growing nicely, investors are happy. But when disruption enters your industry sector, new business models dramatically reset the pricing for traditional services, either by offering a whole lot more for the same price or by offering the same thing for a whole lot less. Either way, your margins are going to take a big hit. Moreover, if you are going to modernize your operating model and then invest in a next-generation disruption of your own, you're going to have to spend working capital to do so, and your margins are going to take an even bigger hit. But here's the thing.

It doesn't have to happen this quarter!

You can postpone it for a while. You still have a lot of legacy customers who would rather pay you a price premium than switch to an unknown entity. You can still squeeze a bit more juice out of the old fruit. To be sure, every quarter a little bit more of your installed base will erode away never to return, and for sure you will not be winning a lot of new customers, but this quarter you can scrape by, defer the reckoning, and collect your current performance bonuses. *How about it?*

Welcome to your crisis of prioritization. If you go for renewal and reinvention, you are likely to alienate your current investors, trash your stock price, and potentially put your company in play. If you opt instead for a path of suppression and denial—what Thoreau once called a "life of quiet desperation"—you are effectively liquidating your company one quarter at a time, all the while keeping up the pretense that you have a viable future. Who do you want to be,

Tweedledum or Tweedledumber? Ugh and ugh! There's one thing for sure: you too are in great need of a new playbook.

A New Playbook

To sum up the foregoing, whether you have been playing offense and trying to catch the next wave or playing defense and trying to defend yourself against a current wave, when it comes to strategic portfolio management, you are likely to need some help. In times of disruption, the current playbook just doesn't work. It does not help us protect our current franchises, nor does it succeed in getting us into new ones. To be frank, we have spent the last several decades acting out Einstein's famous definition of insanity: doing the same thing over and over again and expecting a different result.

At present the situation is so dire that conventional wisdom says established franchises under threat of disruption live on borrowed time. But here is the irony—it should be just the opposite! The advantages that established enterprises have over disruptive startups far outweigh the disadvantages. Global distribution, worldwide support systems, brand recognition, extensive ecosystems, strong balance sheets, predictable cash flow—all these can and should be massively impactful assets. All that is needed is a playbook to focus these resources and leverage them properly. And that is what the chapters that follow intend to provide.

We call this playbook *zone management*. It is based on dividing enterprise management into four zones. Each zone has its own distinctive dynamics—one for revenue performance in the current year, one for productivity initiatives to foster and fuel that performance, one for incubating future innovations, and one for taking such innovations to scale. Each zone follows its own local playbook, each of which will be summarized in the chapters that follow. All four interoperate to enable an established enterprise either to onboard a net new line of business while still maintaining its established franchises or to fend off a disruptive attack on of these same franchises.

None of these four local playbooks is likely to be unfamiliar to you. There are no radical prescriptions in zone management. Rather, what is radical is, first, for executive management to explicitly distribute operations across the four zones and to seek different outcomes within each one, and second, for operational leaders to play within their assigned zones, following the playbook appropriate to each one and collaborating respectfully with other members of the enterprise who are executing different playbooks in other zones.

When you step back from it, it's not all that unlike youth soccer. Like our overenthusiastic children, we all tend to run to the ball, and we all hope to score the goal. But business, like soccer, is a team sport, and success depends on understanding formation and playing position. That is what zone offense and zone defense are all about, in business as in sports.

The foundation for this kind of zone discipline is established in the annual plan. That's where the portfolio decisions are made that determine under which of the four zones' various charters any given initiative is being funded. Once an initiative is "zoned," that establishes the nature of its activity and the metrics upon which it will be evaluated;

it is then the responsibility of the operating staff to execute to those metrics within that zone. The role of the CEO and the executive staff is to allocate resources across the four zones, supervising competition for funding within each one, and orchestrating the interactions across all four. That is, they must explicitly declare first how much will be spent in pursuit of performance, productivity, incubation, and transformation, respectively, then which initiatives should get prioritized within which zones, and finally which inter-zone dependencies need to be monitored most carefully. These ideas are not complicated. But they are powerful.

Specifically, what zone management ensures is that resource allocation, return on investment, organizational structure, operating cadence, success metrics, and management compensation all get aligned with the priorities and deliverables unique to each of the four zones. These are exceptionally powerful levers. In most corporations, unfortunately, they operate at such cross-purposes to one another that it is a wonder the enterprise can perform at all. By contrast, when you disentangle them from conflicting priorities and give each one its own space, the release of creative energy can be breathtaking. You really do hold the keys to the kingdom in your hands. You just have to get them into the right locks.

That's what this playbook is all about.

CHAPTER TWO

The Four Zones

The challenge that zone management seeks to address is triggered when next-generation technology enables new business models to disrupt incumbent franchises. As we have already noted, you can be on either end of this exchange, playing offense as a disruptor or playing defense as a disruptee. That said, whereas the reward for a successful defense is simply stock price *preservation*, the reward for a successful offense is stock price *escalation*, so the ultimate goal is to get on offense sooner or later. Specifically, that means adding a net new line of business to your overall portfolio, one that has revenues greater than 10 percent of total enterprise revenues and is growing at a faster rate. That is the ultimate finish line we are aiming for, regardless of how we get there.

So where is the starting line? The strategic plan is as good a place to start as any, with a specific focus on how best to allocate resources across three *investment horizons.* Each horizon is defined in terms of when the return on that investment will be realized:

- *Horizon 1:* In the coming fiscal year, making it accretive to the operating plan.
- *Horizon 2:* In two to three years, following significant negative cash flow in the intervening period, making it dilutive to the operating plan.
- *Horizon 3:* In three to five years, consisting primarily of research and development that is funded so as not to be dilutive to the operating plan.

In this model the only tangible returns come from Horizon 1. Everything else is speculative at the present time, the intent being to translate it into some Horizon 1 performance in a future year. In this context, Horizon 3 is focused on creating a portfolio of strategic options, and Horizon 2 on translating one or more of those options into a high-performing Horizon 1 asset. Not every Horizon 3 or Horizon 2 initiative is expected to get to Horizon 1 and reach scale, but no material escalation in market valuation will occur until at least one does.

In a non-disrupted sector characterized by evolution and sustaining innovation, Horizon 3 efforts tend to be wide-ranging and exploratory, under little pressure to translate directly into major new lines of business. Most of the time, in other words, there simply aren't any new waves to catch. In this context, Horizon 2 efforts are largely taken up with developing the next generation of products to fill Horizon 1. That is, they are more sustaining than disruptive, so while they are temporarily dilutive, they are relatively low risk, and their long-term contribution is clearly in sight. Overall, therefore, there is a reasonably amicable relationship among all three horizons, funded by ongoing success in Horizon 1. Stock price does not escalate, but it can be maintained and even nudged upward through good management, and at low risk.

All this falls by the wayside when a disruptive business model strikes the sector, typically led by a venture-backed startup with everything to gain and not much to lose. Now every incumbent has just become a potential disruptee. Horizon 1 businesses are under immediate pressure to reform, not so much from direct competitors (although they are always present) as from a new categorical alternative that threatens their very existence. A company like Kodak finds itself fighting not Fuji so much as digital photography; the *Washington Post* not the *New York Times* so much as digital media. This is a new and unfamiliar game, and everyone is definitely playing defense. Under such pressure, executive management turns anxiously to Horizon 3 to find some next-generation technology of their own by which to participate in this new business model, be it coming from its own R&D efforts or from an acquisition, and then mounts an aggressive Horizon 2 effort to bring it to market.

Here, however, its methods fail. Hastily assembled Horizon 3 products and teams are rarely a match for the battle-hardened entrepreneurs and their venture-backed startups with whom the company now competes, and the enterprise team gets little help from its Horizon 1 sales force that is still being compensated to sell the legacy offer set. In addition, this Horizon 2 initiative is consuming cash at a fearsome rate just when Horizon 1 lines of business are struggling to maintain their margins. At some point the CFO calls a time-out during which the company sadly discovers that its best move is actually to retreat from Horizons 2 and 3 altogether and prop up Horizon 1 margins with some deep cost cutting. In the short term a reckoning has been deferred, but the existential threat has by no means been addressed, and the company's power has been further eroded. The end result over time is an inexorable marginalizing of the business and its brand, ultimately culminating in a period of consolidating acquisitions among last-generation legacy franchises—a poor defense indeed.

This is the norm, but it is not a desirable outcome, so it is important to note that there is another way, a way to break free from this kind of downward spiral. Indeed, there is a clear path to deflecting the current disruption and ultimately becoming a disruptor rather than a disruptee. That is what this playbook purports to describe. At its core is a simple idea based on the observation that startups routinely outperform incumbents in disrupted markets. How come? *Because they are not conflicted.* All their enemies are outside them. Incumbent enterprises, on the other hand, are pulled in multiple directions, not just by their own economic interests and those of their shareholders but by those of their customers and partner ecosystems as well. Torn by these forces, their efforts lack focus and prioritization, and it is little wonder they fall short of the mark.

To compete effectively, management must free itself from this bind. It needs to reconfigure its enterprise to fight independently on multiple fronts, acting in parallel but not in lockstep. Specifically, it needs to segregate its efforts in *disruptive innovation* from those in *sustaining innovation*, focusing the former on net new business and operating models and the latter on extensions and improvements to existing ones. At the same time, it needs to separate its *revenue performance* activities from its *enabling investments*, focusing the former on delivering results based on what the latter have helped to seed and till.

As the following diagram indicates, these two divisions result in four zones of management activity, each aligned with one, and only one, investment horizon, each demanding a different style of leadership to achieve those ends.

The Four Zones

	Disruptive Innovation	Sustaining Innovation
Revenue Performance	TRANSFORMATION ZONE Horizon 2	PERFORMANCE ZONE Horizon 1
Enabling Investments	INCUBATION ZONE Horizon 3	PRODUCTIVITY ZONE Horizon 1

The sustaining side of this model is the home of established franchises and their operating models, the return-on-investment focus being on Horizon 1. Their revenue performance obligation is to "make the number," and they are supported in doing so by a variety of enabling investments in shared services. The disruptive side, by contrast, is the domain of emerging businesses. They are gestated as a set of enabling investments in Horizon 3, where fast failure is often a virtue. When it is time to choose one of these to bring to scale, however, management takes on a mission-critical obligation to generate revenue at a material level, nominally 10 percent or more of total enterprise top line, thereby embracing the challenge of Horizon 2.

The differences among zones in terms of investment horizon, performance metrics, and operating cadence are so great that each warrants its own local playbook, with no zone being permitted to impose its local playbook onto any of the other three. At the same time, however, all four zones do need to interoperate with each other fluidly if the overall enterprise is to win the game. Thus, there does need to be an overarching playbook to govern them all, what for disruptors we will be calling *zone offense*, for disruptees, *zone defense*.

With all this in mind, here is a thumbnail sketch of each of the four zones.

The Performance Zone

Beginning at twelve o'clock and proceeding clockwise, we come first to the performance zone. This is the engine room for operating established franchises on proven business models. The focus is on material revenue performance derived from established businesses that are *sustaining* to the status quo. It is home to the organizations that make the offers you sell and sell the offers you make. These are people who pride themselves on delivering the goods—on time, on spec, and on budget—and making the number—quarter after quarter after quarter. They are all about the operating model, and they are all about performance.

When an enterprise voluntarily embraces business model disruption in a proactive attempt to add a net new line of business to its Horizon 1 portfolio, it puts enormous stress on the performance zone. Not only must the zone deliver on revenue commitments to the established lines of business, it must also help drive the transformation of an incubation zone business to material scale. As we shall discuss at length, this creates issues around resource allocation, core talent, competing products, and mixed marketing messages that require innovative responses to manage.

By contrast, when an enterprise is involuntarily disrupted by an outsider with a new business model attacking its established franchise, then it must set aside any disruptive ideas of its own and mobilize its performance zone to fight off the new challenge. Its primary tactic here is to revitalize its established business model by modernizing its operating model as fast as possible, ideally by co-opting some of the same technology that the disruptor is using to gain its competitive advantage. In this scenario the enterprise is still making and selling what it used to, but the way it is doing so is being rapidly reengineered. Once again, this puts enormous stress on the performance zone and puts revenue goal attainment at risk because everyone is much less productive for the duration of the learning curves involved.

The importance of maintaining the viability of the performance zone can hardly be overstated. It is the source of more than 90 percent of the enterprise's revenues and well north of 100 percent of its profits. Its health is measured by financial operating ratios, resource allocation hurdles, performance metrics, and the like. The return-on-investment focus is always Horizon 1, with results being published quarterly in the company's financial reports.

The fact that financial investors scrutinize these reports so intensely, however, has given rise to the mistaken conclusion that quarterly performance is all shareholders care about, and that therefore Horizon 1 mandates—and by consequence the performance zone's local playbook—should be prioritized above all others. Meeting the number is incredibly important, but it cannot be sacrosanct. Making it so blocks the transformational commitment necessary to add any net new lines of business. It makes zone offense a complete nonstarter and leads inexorably to a slow and steady harvesting of the enterprise's good will and brand power. So as mission-critical as the performance zone is, it is still only one of four and must be managed as such for modern business success.

The Productivity Zone

The productivity zone is home to a host of enabling investments in shared services, all managed as cost centers. These include marketing, central engineering, technical support, manufacturing, supply chain, customer service, human resources, IT, legal, finance, and administration. Simply put, any function in the corporation that does not have direct accountability for a material revenue number goes here. The focus is on applying sustaining innovation to productivity-enabling initiatives targeted primarily at the performance zone with the bulk of the ROI expected to fall into Horizon 1. These initiatives are delivered via programs and systems for ensuring regulatory compliance, efficient operations, and effective competitive performance. The normal challenge for the productivity zone is to manage the tensions among its three core deliverables—compliance, efficiency, and effectiveness—without subordinating any one of them to the other two. This becomes even more challenging during a period of operating model disruption because the performance zone heightens its demands for both efficiency and effectiveness while bridling at constraints imposed in support of compliance. This is the challenge of zone defense. It can become even more challenging still when the transformation zone puts the entire enterprise on notice to prioritize its next-wave efforts. This is the challenge of zone offense. Shared-services organizations that have gotten comfortable, not to say complacent, during less stressful periods are often bewildered by these new circumstances and question how much they really need to change. Well, as Deming once said, "Change is not necessary because survival is not mandatory." If the enterprise is going to succeed in times like these, the productivity zone is going to need a new playbook as well.

The Incubation Zone

On the disruptive side of the ledger, the incubation zone plays enabling host to fast-growing offers in emerging categories and markets that are not yet producing a material amount of revenue. Its charter is a simple one: Position the enterprise to catch the next wave. This is the domain of Horizon 3, where any significant return on investment is several years out, and revenues for this zone's portfolio are in aggregate no more than a percent or two of the enterprise's total top line.

That said, in a Fortune 500 company, this can still amount to hundreds of millions of dollars, so we should not think of these as just skunkworks. Rather, they are simply an order of magnitude or more too small to participate productively in the operating model of the performance zone. That's why the two zones need to be isolated from one another.

In the incubation zone the difference between playing offense and defense is stark. On offense, the game begins when one (and only one) incubating business is sent to the transformation zone for scaling. We'll discuss its fate when we get to that zone in a minute. In the meantime, all but the most nascent of the other businesses in the incubation zone have to reposition themselves for some alternative exit. Access to the transformation zone is going to be closed for the foreseeable future, likely the next two to three years, and for most business opportunities that is simply too long to wait. How to negotiate these exits is something we will go into further detail in a later chapter.

By contrast, when the enterprise is playing defense, all the focus goes to the performance zone. One of its first moves is to scour the incubation zone for any technology that can help it modernize its operating model to fend off the disruptive attack. In this context, technology that was once envisioned as a platform for proactively disrupting someone else's business model is now converted into a tool for reactively propping up one's own. The fledgling business that was incubating this technology is now subordinated to the needs of the established business, and its crown jewels are appropriated and assimilated into the latter's product road map to give it the necessary boost to fight off the disruptor. To say the least, this was not the dream that motivated the incubating team, so it is important to take the time to secure buy-in to the situation at hand.

Overall, come offense or defense, in an age of disruption, our whole approach to innovation needs to be refashioned. We must rethink how to fund and manage following a venture model inside a publicly held corporation, how to identify and transition the strongest candidate to the transformation zone, how to support a performance zone under pressure and keep people focused and motivated at the same time, and how to manage the disposition of the many incubated businesses that do not get backed for scale. It makes for a very interesting new playbook indeed.

The Transformation Zone

The transformation zone is the place in an established enterprise where a disruptive business model goes to be scaled to material size. It is primarily a tool for offense, the goal being to scale rapidly to a stable, material, net new line of business, one that constitutes 10 percent or more of the enterprise's current revenues, on a growth trajectory that promises both increased size and superior profitability. To win you must catch a wave of next-generation technology just as it is entering its secular growth phase and then put the full force of your global go-to-market capability behind it. The challenge here is that the both the category and the business itself are immature and subscale, so when you put the full power of the performance zone to work, the early results are not encouraging. Indeed, until you are clearly past the tipping point, virtually every force inside and outside your company will be working against you. Nonetheless, this is the course you have chosen, and you must not abandon it.

In zone defense, there is another kind of transformational goal—to reengineer the operating model of one or more businesses in the performance zone to ward off the attack of a disruptor. The reason the transformation zone has to get involved here is that, left to its own devices, the performance zone will just keep on performing. The existing management team is simply too entrenched in its established ways, too indebted to the current ecosystem, too implicated in the web of favors that holds any industry together over the long haul, to drive a disruptive change. These are the people who built this franchise. You cannot ask them to lead its dismantling. But dismantle it you must if you are going to have any chance of fending off the disruptor at your gates. So as with zone offense, the CEO must step in, reset the priorities across all four zones, anoint the one line of business whose needs will come before all others, and drive the repel-the-disruption initiative until the franchise restabilizes.

The return-on-investment period for all transformation zone efforts is Horizon 2. This means that all transformation initiatives, whether on offense or defense, inevitably entail a J-curve wherein performance metrics go south before they turn the corner to go north. Such a trajectory is unavoidable since any disruption at the business-model level inevitably entails reengineering the underlying operating model, which in turn mandates reengineering the supporting infrastructure model. Overall, this makes for a huge change-management problem. J-curves are never easy to manage, but they are exceptionally challenging for a publicly held company whose investors have grown used to steady growth from well-established, profitable lines of business. This puts excruciating stress on the performance zone's operating model to both make its mission-critical sustaining commitments and assimilate a mission-critical disruption. There is no avoiding the nasty bit that ensues, and if the CEO loses control of the transformation narrative, odds are the initiative will get derailed long before the finish line.

All told, transformation is a time when any principle of conventional management wisdom may not be just wrong but fatal. Force-feeding a new business model into the performance zone or reengineering an existing operating model to give a legacy business a new lease on life are both fundamentally unnatural acts. Of all the four playbooks needed to make the four zones model work, this is the one that requires the greatest amount of creative rethinking.

Zone Management

Even from this cursory review of the four zones, it should be clear that their individual goals, objectives, and methods are so diverse that any set of management methods creating success in one zone is likely to cause failure in the other three. That is why it is so important to keep them separate. At the same time, all four need to work in tandem to make the corporation go. Here's how a successfully "zoned-up" company operates:

- The performance zone is the primary focus of the senior operating team, with an emphasis on steady management as opposed to bold leadership. The CEO is present and engaged, but for the most part the company is run at the next level down, following the objectives and budgets laid out in the annual operating plan, with a lot of attention paid to execution metrics. The goal is to be a well-oiled machine that produces good risk-adjusted returns with few surprises. This is your revenue engine.

- The productivity zone spends most of its time targeting efficiencies to be gained by improving operations in the performance zone. Its primary goal is to extract resources from noncore work—what we call context—in order to either invest more in core tasks or take the savings to the bottom line. This is your earnings engine. If the performance zone's job is to make the top line, the productivity zone's job is to help make the bottom line. The two should work hand in glove.

- The incubation zone will have a number of things cooking at any given point in time. Each will have been funded based on its potential to catch the next big wave—there are no resources wasted on "interesting" projects that have no clear path to scale. M&A is active and includes the onboarding of next-generation technology teams. Also at any given point in time, one or more of these efforts is likely to be showing signs that it is ready to transition to full scale. This is your candidate pool for playing offense. At the same time, in the event of a disruptive attack on your core lines of business, it is also a contingency pool for playing defense.

- Because transformations are expensive, risky, and exhausting, in most years the transformation zone is likely to be empty. This is actually a desirable state because it means that the enterprise can have another productive year creating attractive returns at relatively low risk. Remember, you need only to succeed in one transformative initiative per decade to be world-class. That transformation is likely to take three years and be brutally painful, so you will want plenty of time both to reap its rewards and recover from the experience.

When the transformation zone does become activated in service to a zone offense initiative, this puts the whole enterprise on red alert. The CEO is at the helm, hand directly on the tiller. This is the time for bold leadership, with prudent management just having to hold on for dear life. You have put a single opportunity into the chute. All other potential disruptions have been put on hold. The entire executive team must be obsessed with getting this net new line of business past the tipping point of contributing 10 percent or more of total enterprise revenue. You will not be denied.

Alternatively, when a disruptive attack demands a zone defense to repel it, the transformation zone will also kick into action, once again putting the whole enterprise on red alert, this time focusing everyone on modernizing the established operating model to participate successfully in the new era. During this effort there will be no attempt to play zone offense as there is not enough resource to do both, and for an established enterprise, preserving the core business takes priority.

Overall, the four zones should always be operating in

harmony. During periods of stability, when the transformation zone is dormant, the performance zone is funding the entire operation, with help from the productivity zone, paving the way for the incubation zone, building up whatever reserves it can for the next transformation. During a zone offense, the transformation zone rules the roost, its priorities trumping all others, with the performance zone coming in second, the productivity zone third, and the incubation zone last. The same priorities hold for zone defense, the main difference being that the focus is not on adding a new business but rather on ensuring that an existing one does not get subtracted. Both offense and defense put the enterprise under significant stress, so everyone in all four zones should wake up every morning asking themselves, "What can we do today to accelerate the transformation initiative?" This isn't just altruism. It is also pain relief.

That's what good looks like. Unfortunately, historically it has shown up far too infrequently. So what is likely to be happening instead? Following the traditional management playbook, executive teams typically commit the following kinds of errors:

- *Overrotating to the performance zone.* Investors scrutinize quarterly financials, and the executive compensation plan is designed to pay for performance, so it is only natural to allocate additional resources to this zone. This is fine so long as there is no transformational initiative in play. Once there is, however, it is critical to overrotate to the transformation zone. Letting the performance zone keep to its current course and speed is a showstopper.

- *Coasting in the productivity zone.* Initiatives in this zone are for the most part neither disruptive nor mission-critical, so it is easy to get a bit complacent about performance here. Again, absent a transformational initiative, all you're likely to be giving up are a few hundred basis points of EPS. But once a transformation is under way, you will put so much pressure on the performance zone that the only way you can succeed is with an exceptional contribution from your enabling initiatives. If the productivity zone is not up to the task, you are not going to get up to the bar.

- *Mistaking the incubation zone for the transformation zone.* This is one-half of a classic portfolio management mistake. Anxiety about not catching the next wave causes everyone to focus on businesses in the incubation zone, hoping that one will bust out in all its glory and save the day. This is a fantasy. The actual path to success demands much more sacrifice, the sort of thing that can only be made possible in the transformation zone.

- *Failing to implement a transformation zone.* This is the other half of the portfolio management mistake. The strategy of maintaining multiple options leads inevitably to undertaking more than one transformation at a time, each under the purview of a senior executive, none specifically privileged by the CEO. The ensuing scramble for resources results in no transformational initiative getting anything like the prioritization it needs to succeed. The end result is a discouraging sequence of marginalized initiatives, each too small to make any difference to investors, each too big to just shut down and walk away from. After a painfully prolonged twilight existence, these usually end up getting tucked into one or another established line of business where they are gradually dissolved into the legacy product feature set. As T. S. Eliot once wrote, it all ends "not with a bang but a whimper."

- *Falling prey to denial when faced with a disruptive attack.* Borders when faced with Amazon, Nokia when faced with Apple, Yahoo! when faced with Google—when an enterprise has been so successful for so long, it is easy to fall prey to a sense of entitlement that simply rejects the possibility of an upstart holding sway. Then as the upstart gains more and more ground, internally it becomes politically challenging to hold the tough conversations needed to drive a corrective response. In such situations the current management playbook would have one stay the course with the old guard occupying the key management positions, but experience has shown that it is virtually impossible for the company to make an effective response under those conditions.

In sum, when faced with a wave of disruptive technology, be it as an opportunity or a threat, current playbooks do not serve management well. To remediate this state of affairs there are three essential steps that must be taken:

1. Install a governance model that segregates the four zones from one another. In particular, do not let the methods, metrics, or culture of the performance

zone infiltrate the governance of either the incubation or the transformation zone.

2. Establish and implement best practices in each zone independently (including how it interfaces with the other three). This includes establishing which offerings and initiatives are being managed out of which zones and making concomitant adjustments to their goals, objectives, methods, metrics, and governance models.

3. Overlay a lightweight corporate system to oversee all four zones in parallel. All the real work is done within each of the four zones, but annual planning, resource allocation, and the quarterly business reviews need to be managed across all four while keeping each distinct from the other three.

These three imperatives shape the playbook that follows. In each of the next four chapters we will lay out the management framework for one of the four zones and then, taking a page from the "faults and fixes" segments in golf magazines, highlight some of the most common mistakes made in that zone and how best to address them. In effect, each chapter will provide a local playbook for operating inside that zone, the goal being to create maximum clarity and alignment for superior execution within that context.

Then we will step back to look at how all four zones are best managed in tandem as management confronts each of our three disruption scenarios—no disruption (half time), proactively attacking via disruption (zone offense), and reactively defending against disruption (zone defense). This will include a section on how to zone to win by installing zone discipline during the annual planning process. Then we will close with two case studies, the first featuring Salesforce playing offense, the second featuring Microsoft playing defense. After that, you will be on your own.

CHAPTER THREE

The Performance Zone

The performance zone generates virtually all the revenue and more than 100 percent of the profits of the enterprise. It consists of a portfolio of lines of business, each with an established installed base. Revenue growth overall is typically cyclical, normally oscillating around 3 to 4 percent in mature categories, a bit higher in the newer ones. Within any given sector, market shares are relatively stable, distributed among a cohort of competitors, all more or less contemporaries, and while there is always the potential threat of disruption, these categories at present are characterized by evolution, not revolution. Think gasoline-powered automobiles, fast-food restaurants, industrial equipment, management consulting, hospitals and clinics, and insurance.

In short, we are on Main Street—no early market experiments, no chasms to cross, perhaps some niche market development programs to capitalize on the granularity of growth, but no tornadoes driving massive secular shifts in spending. Main Street is home to the bulk of the world's business, the preponderance of its jobs, the foundations of its tax revenues. Its health is our health, and the watchword is "Steady as she goes." Management's goal here is to maximize yields while not screwing things up. Play hard, play fair, and root out all forms of corruption aggressively. Optimize for the present, but invest enough to maintain the franchise.

Strategies on Main Street are relatively easy to frame, typically prioritizing either operational excellence or customer intimacy, with product leadership being a distant third. It is a world where, for many, good enough is good enough, so you had better either delight your customer or show up with the best price. In either case the main challenge is execution, and that is where the *performance matrix* comes in.

A performance matrix is an organizational model optimized for managing a portfolio of established franchises across a single shared go-to-market fabric. It segments the field of execution into rows and columns, the rows representing a set of business lines, each of which operates at scale, the columns a set of go-to-market channels through which this set of offers is sold, again at scale. *Scale* here means greater than 10 percent of total enterprise revenue, a threshold of materiality designed to make the overall matrix both effective and efficient. Applying this standard, a typical performance matrix consists of somewhere between three and six rows intersecting with three to six columns.

Here's a typical illustration from a B2B enterprise that sells direct to other businesses.

The Performance Matrix

Column Owners
Channels of Revenue (Sales)

Row Owners
Sources of Revenue (BUs)

						TOTAL
						TOTAL
						TOTAL
						TOTAL
						TOTAL
						TOTAL
TOTAL	TOTAL	TOTAL	TOTAL	TOTAL	TOTAL	**TOTAL**

Targeted Revenue, Bookings, Growth Rate & Contribution Margin

Joint Accountability of Every Cell
"Interlock"

In this model rows and columns are each assigned unique owners who are accountable for the business results from every cell in their row or column. Cell-level results are measured primarily in terms of bookings, revenues, and contribution margins, with additional attention paid to churn, growth, market share, and customer satisfaction, as warranted. At the cell level, row-oriented programs are focused on delivering the product/service road map on time, on spec, and on budget, and column-oriented programs on developing and processing a pipeline of sales opportunities at an appropriate rate, volume, and yield. Overall, the performance matrix is a data-driven affair: it's all about *performance metrics* driving an *operating cadence*.

The operating cadence is set by the annual operating plan, subdivided by quarter, creating the context for quarterly business reviews. These will focus on areas that are significantly behind plan, the key question being do we double down on our current efforts or change course? Course changes can be grouped into three kinds under the mnemonic *horse, rider, trail.* That is, if our current plan is failing and we want to make a change, should we swap out the horse (the product or service we are offering), the rider (the manager in charge of the function that is underperforming), or the trail (the market segment we are targeting)? Most plans and organizations can absorb one change per year. Few can tolerate two.

Limited elasticity to absorb change makes it critical to nip underperforming outcomes in the bud. This drives monthly status checks where row and column owners review their matrix of cells on a red/yellow/green basis, the goal being to detect and address problems quickly. That spirit in turn drives a locally managed work culture of weekly commits. These commits are highly variable in content, reflecting whatever is currently on the critical path. The point is to identify what those things are and focus attention immediately on addressing those issues. Under performance pressure, schedules are the first thing to slip, but in a weekly commits culture, nothing can slip for more than one week without getting escalated.

Governance

In terms of governance, setting aside the bottommost row and right-hand column (the ones labeled *TOTALS*), every cell in the performance matrix has two owners, each of whom is held jointly accountable with the other for achieving that cell's metrics. Joint accountability is established during the annual planning process, where both owners must sign off on a single set of metrics, which will in turn be reviewed and approved by the CFO, the CEO, and the board of directors.

Maintaining a standard of scale in the performance matrix can be a challenge. Both product lines and sales territory geographies can get offended when you call out their status as subscale. But in reality they should welcome it because under the current dynamics they will be underserved. Instead, they should seek one of two alternative treatments. If they expect to participate in secular growth in the relatively near future, then they should seek incubation zone status, where they can be governed by a highly empowered GM who can make the quick calls needed to capitalize on rapidly changing market conditions—riding the next wave. Alternatively, if they expect to see cyclical growth, then they should aggregate with other subscale entities or join forces with a larger, established one to get the scale necessary to warrant the attention they need. Subsisting at subscale indefinitely is a losing game.

Playing Offense in the Performance Zone

The goal of zone offense is to add a net new row to the performance matrix. This effort is driven out of the transformation zone, but much of the heavy lifting has to be done by the performance matrix. Here's what's involved.

The fledgling business has to be scaled to material size within a finite window of opportunity—typically three years or less—*no matter what!* At the same time, the perennial charter of the performance zone is to make the annual number— *no matter what!* At the end of the day, you cannot have two number-one priorities, and here is where most established enterprises go astray. When it comes time to choose, they default to making the number. This is a mistake.

The correct response is to put completing the transformation first. Here's why:

- Catching a wave of disruptive innovation is a time-critical undertaking. You cannot go back—there are no do-overs.
- Transformation is a temporary undertaking, which, if successful, will restore an underperforming performance zone to superior returns in future years.
- Making the number is still a top priority—second only to making the transformation itself, so it trumps all other initiatives the enterprise may have under way. If we do miss our number, we do not intend to miss it by much.

With significant help from the productivity zone, the number can still be made. It's just going to take a lot of creativity and commitment to do so.

The best analogy for this overall situation is how a professional sports league supports an expansion team. Eventually everyone in the league is going to profit from adding the new team, but in the short term every existing team has to give up resources to launch the new effort. In the performance matrix this equates to staffing and funding the transformational initiative on a no-compromise basis, even if that means reassigning talent you were counting on to make the base plan. This sacrifice is made even more painful by the fact that the new category is subscale and does not perform anywhere near as well as the mature ones in the short term. Moreover, matrix leaders must defer to the transformation zone as well when it comes to productivity zone resource allocation—again, even when this delays programs they were counting on to help make their number.

One of the key levers established enterprises can bring to bear on offense, one where they have a clear advantage, is their ability to redirect their professional services organization to prioritize projects that impact the transformation zone. These organizations operate at a scale that startups can only dream of. The key is to take advantage of this capability to accelerate the race to scale and not to let the organization get tied down making its revenue commitments to the performance matrix. Yes, those commitments are important too, but not as much as driving a successful transformation. That trumps everything else.

Given all these adjustments to standard operating procedure, in a time of transformation it is critical to revamp the success metrics for the performance matrix leaders to make sure they are aligned with the new corporate priorities. For the established cells, this means adjusting the values in the old metrics to acknowledge the additional pressure being put on the zone. For the new cells, it means setting out a very different set of metrics, one heavily weighted toward rapid revenue growth, steadily improving gross margins, and increasingly dominant market share in the new category. It is tricky to manage different cells to qualitatively different targets, hence the need for the CEO to take an active role in leading the transformation. But if the metrics are clear, consistent, and fair, performance organizations can and will perform.

Playing Defense in the Performance Zone

The focus of zone offense is on becoming a disruptor yourself, catching a next-generation technology wave and riding it to add a new earnings engine to your enterprise portfolio and a whopping increase in market valuation. That is the big payoff for successfully navigating the transformation zone. But what do you do when you are not the disruptor but instead the disruptee? How, in other words, does one play zone defense?

The first principle of zone defense is that you must never attempt to disrupt yourself. As an established enterprise, your number-one asset is the inertial momentum of your installed customer base. Your number-two asset is an ecosystem of partners that makes its living adding value to your established offerings. These are amazing assets, the very things that the disruptor covets for itself, and you must never abandon them, never break faith with either constituency. So when consultants tell you that you have to disrupt yourself, tell them to get lost. Successful disruptors disrupt other companies' businesses, not their own.

The second principle of zone defense is to focus your R&D innovation on *neutralization*, not *differentiation*. This is the opposite of the disruptors' strategy. They have to differentiate—it's the only way they can win your customers away from you. You, on the other hand, do not. You are the incumbent, the default choice, with inertia on your side. What you do have to do, however, is respond to the disruption in a timely manner. You cannot go into denial and bury your head in the sand.

Specifically, you have to co-opt some portion of the

disruptive innovation and integrate it into your established offering. The result does not have to be best in class. It has to be good enough. That is, it has to allow customers and partners to get enough benefit from a combination of old and new to make your overall deal better than one they would get from the disruptor. That's the basis of your defense. You are showing them a road map to the future while maintaining their existing asset base.

The third and final principle of zone defense is to appropriate whatever incubation zone assets you have in the works that pertain to the new technology and put them directly in service to the established business under attack. This entails abandoning any thought of pursuing the original zone offense play—the external disruptor has already beat you to that punch. Instead, focus on integrating this technology into your mature offering so as to give the latter a midlife kicker, providing to your customers and partners expanded capability that is compatible with their current infrastructure. This is not a perfect solution, to be sure. The technology gap between old and new is likely to be severe, and the integration solution is likely to be considerably less than elegant. This means you are incurring a substantial technology debt, one you will have to pay down over time going forward. But it blunts the disruptor's progress at the point of attack just at the time when it matters most, so strategically, it gets high marks.

A good case study for this is Microsoft's response to Netscape Navigator, the web browser that dramatically disrupted its Windows franchise back in the mid-1990s. The company did not abandon Windows. Instead, it quickly cobbled together a browser of its own, Internet Explorer

1.0, which was, truth be told, a pretty bad product. But they were back in the game, and by the time it came to release 3.0, it was a very good product. More importantly, it came integrated into Windows at no extra charge. The strategy worked, Internet Explorer became the default browser for Windows, and Netscape's disruption was beaten back.

Subsequently, however, Microsoft neglected to sustain its innovation investment in its browser in the decade following, allowing first Mozilla's Firefox and then Google's Chrome to pass it by. Today, its position has been dangerously eroded at a time when Windows on devices is becoming less consequential and HTLM5 browsing more so. It is working to address this issue with its new Edge browser for Windows 10, but this was an unforced error—it need never have happened—and we should all learn from it.

Faults and Fixes

- *Failure to secure interlock at the cell level.* The most common mistake in implementing a performance matrix is to hold sales channels accountable to the total number for their column but not for each of the specific cells that make up that column. This seems reasonable enough—money is money, after all—until you realize it leaves the product/service row owners completely in the lurch. They have no mechanism by which to hold the field accountable to their particular offer set. In times of disruption, when every business unit is under pressure to deliver, this is simply unacceptable. It is absolutely mandatory to enforce cell-level accountability across all sales channels, not only during the annual planning process but also in the quarterly business reviews and monthly status updates. A cell-accountable matrix makes a great dashboard that lets everyone know every month how every part of the business is doing.

- *Driving cell-level interlock responsibility too low in the sales organization.* This is the opposite mistake from the previous one. Here you have enforced accountability at too granular a level. Some territories and some account teams simply are not set up to sell certain offers, and not all offers are suited to all channels. Managers in the middle of the sales organization must have the discretion to modify accountability at the local level while at the same time maintaining it at the aggregate level. Make sure your CRM system gives them the flexibility needed to do this and that your compensation program does not punish them for doing so.

- *Failing to maintain a disciplined execution cadence.* The performance matrix requires constant supervision. As we have already mentioned, best practice is to conduct weekly commits at the departmental level with monthly status updates and quarterly business reviews at the division level. The goal is to jump on any cell that has turned yellow or red and "get it to green" as quickly as possible. Shortfalls in performance normally manifest themselves first as slipped schedule commitments, and the only realistic chances for remediation depend on early detection and immediate response.

- *Allowing subscale rows or columns into the matrix.* It is fruitless to negotiate an interlock with a subscale partner. If you achieve the number, it won't move the needle, and if you fail, no one will take an interest in remedying the situation. All you will have done is suck up a lot of people's time while weakening the power of the matrix as a whole. Once any row or column in the matrix escapes accountability, the whole mechanism loses its force.

  To correct this fault, first remove from the performance matrix any businesses that are in the incubation zone. They simply do not belong in the performance zone because their high cost of sales, long sales cycles, and relatively small initial deal sizes all mitigate against making the number. Instead, they are going to get a completely separate go-to-market treatment outboard of the performance matrix. For the remaining businesses, ones that are mature but subscale, insist that they either aggregate with each other or integrate with other product or service lines in order to get to scale. Every entity in the matrix, be it a row-based offer or a column-based sales channel, must subtotal to 10 percent or more of total revenue. Scale is sacrosanct.

- *Assigning row-level responsibility to product line managers instead of general managers.* This often goes hand in hand with allowing subscale rows into the matrix. In addition to creating a matrix of unmanageable size and complexity, it assigns execution responsibility to a role that is too junior to wield the authority necessary to hold the rest of the enterprise accountable to a given row or cell's success. It is not only sales executives who must be held accountable for sales commits; success also depends on holding program leaders in shared services like marketing, engineering, and the supply chain to their enabling commitments as well. It really does take a village to make a number in a performance matrix cell, and only a senior executive operating with the authority of a general manager has the clout to orchestrate this effort properly.

- *Incentivizing professional services to maximize revenue growth.* For companies that earn the preponderance of their revenues via a product or licensed service model, professional services create considerably more value spearheading next-generation offers for competitive advantage than they do delivering financial performance via their own operations. That's because they are critical to winning early adopters for next-generation offers that are always bought as services-led projects. Furthermore, later on in the life cycle professional services can accelerate mainstream market adoption by packaging up their expertise to train and empower third parties in the ecosystem. In this context it is usually much better to modulate professional services organizations' revenue targets, still keeping them above 10 percent of total revenue so that the performance matrix functions properly but not allowing them to get to 20 percent. That is, you can still give these organizations revenue and contribution margin targets to hit, but the primary focus should be on increasing the power of the performance zone to win next-generation deals as opposed to just supplementing its financial performance.

• *Allocating corporate overhead to rows and columns in the performance matrix.* The matrix is not a P&L—it is an operational construct. In that context, it is appropriate to hold row and column owners accountable for their *controllable* indirect expenses. These consist of shared services consumed directly in the pursuit of their financial objectives, such as marketing programs, subsidized professional services, or outsourced development, testing, or integration. All this is fair game to allocate to the matrix of row and column owners.

By contrast, holding these same matrix leaders accountable for *overhead* expenses over which they have no discretionary say is simply a mistake. It just drives them crazy and causes ceaseless arguments over seemingly arbitrary allocations that are highly material to their objectives and compensation. Moreover, it is a cop-out on the part of the productivity zone leaders themselves, including the CFO, who need to either "sell" these services to the matrix in some form of a controllable indirect expense or take direct cost-center responsibility for them as necessary overhead. Shuffling this burden off onto others is bad form.

Concluding Remarks

Overall, when operating in nondisrupted markets, enterprises can make any number of these mistakes and still perform well financially. This is testimony to the power of inertia. It works so much to the incumbents' advantage that discipline can be lax without jeopardizing success. Sure, all the numbers could be a little better, but the customers aren't going anywhere, and we can get that money next quarter. Chill out.

The reckoning, of course, comes with the advent of a disruptive innovation. Now the enterprise finds itself painfully out of position, with its performance matrix leaders lacking the skills, the discipline, and often the courage to take on the new challenge. Making changes in personnel at this point is risky and dangerous, but not making them is usually fatal. You simply must not let your enterprise drift into this state. Even if you are not under a current threat of disruption, you need to assume you will be soon and use the intervening period to get yourself into fighting shape.

To do so, reassert a set of disciplines that, truth be told, are simply best practices at any time:

1. Base the annual operating plan for the performance zone on financial metrics optimized for maximizing returns in the current fiscal year, what we have been calling Horizon 1.
2. Organize operations around the rows and columns of the performance matrix, assigning a unique owner to each row and column, empowering that owner to be a single point of accountability for both making and meeting the plan.
3. Aggregate operational units such that no row or column represents less than 10 percent of the revenues of the overall operating plan.

4. If a zone offense transformation is being undertaken, add a net new *subscale* row to the performance matrix, and then scale it as fast as possible. If a zone defense transformation is being undertaken, identify the row that is under attack, reset its metrics, and reprioritize its resource allocation to get it back into fighting shape, again as fast as possible.

5. Secure explicit interlock commitments for each of the performance metrics in every cell from the row owner and column owner directly involved, to be ratified by the CFO and the CEO, who will then review it with the board of directors.

6. Conduct quarterly business reviews in which all row and column owners must be present to speak to the current state of their businesses. These are command performances and should not be rescheduled to accommodate other pressing demands.

7. Install a cadence of weekly commits and monthly status updates to drive both a data-driven and a date-driven approach to making the number.

These are the key principles. As you can see, they are neither novel nor radical. They simply require a firm commitment to discipline. And that, after all, is what the performance zone is all about.

CHAPTER FOUR

The Productivity Zone

In business, without revenue, you are dead in the water, so management attention is naturally drawn first to the performance zone. That said, you had better pay attention to the productivity zone as well if you want to take any of that money home with you at the end of the day. Put another way, if it is the performance zone's job to win the war at the top line, it is the productivity zone's job to win the peace at the bottom line.

The productivity zone is home to all enterprise resources that do not have direct accountability for revenue in any of the three horizons. Organized as a set of shared services provided by professionals who are experts in their particular disciplines, it includes the following functions:

- *Core corporate:* Finance, Accounting, Legal, Business Development, Investor Relations, Administration,

Facilities, Information Technology, Human Relations, Training, and the like.

- *Market facing:* Marketing, Communications, Lead Generation, Customer Service, Order Processing, Customer Support, and the like.
- *Supply chain facing:* Central Engineering, Manufacturing, Purchasing, Transportation and Logistics, Quality, Technical Support, and the like.

The purpose of all these organizations is to enable the enterprise to operate as productively as possible. They do so by delivering on one or more of the following value propositions:

1. Regulatory compliance
2. Improved efficiency ("doing things right")
3. Improved effectiveness ("doing the right things")

All three entail enabling disciplines that are outboard of the core performance of the enterprise but integral to its overall economic success. At the same time, each goal is so different from the other two, in both methods and intent, as to require separate and distinct management. Most management teams understand that regulatory compliance warrants a separate track, but few recognize the importance of separating efficiency from effectiveness, something we will address directly in just a moment.

With respect to regulatory compliance, this is the tax enterprises must pay for the freedoms and privileges of operating under rule of law. The breadth and depth of this effort varies considerably by both geography and industry sector, but the spirit it should always be the same. Company culture, values, and tone at the top are the driving engines of compliance; oversight, detection, and remediation are the course-correcting activities. As with quality, you cannot *inspect* compliance in; you have to *design* it in and then monitor it vigilantly.

Consider that the high road. If you take any other, or find yourself unexpectedly off course, you are in for a lot of very painful work. There is simply no easy way out of a compliance mess, so it behooves you to take serious steps to make sure you don't get into one. This is the purview of the audit committee of the board of directors, the external auditors, the internal audit function, and the chief compliance officer, all supported by an executive team communicating respect for the principles and support for the processes involved. It is not complicated. It is just not negotiable.

That all said, regulatory compliance absorbs a very small fraction of the resources expended in the productivity zone. The bulk go instead to driving improvements in efficiency and effectiveness. As previously noted, these are two very different objectives. The former is properly the province of *systems*, the latter of *programs*, and it is critical to keep these two practice areas separate and distinct. A look at the table below shows the reasons why:

SYSTEMS	PROGRAMS
Excel at creating efficiency	Excel at creating effectiveness
Should be standard or configurable	Should be custom or customizable
Stable and persistent	Adaptable and timely

SYSTEMS	PROGRAMS
Enterprise priorities come first	Participant priorities come first
Centrally funded, top-down adoption	Consumer-funded, bottom-up adoption
Challenged to be flexible	Challenged to be scalable

Systems are services that provide ongoing operational infrastructure. Corporate-funded systems include the annual budgeting process, payroll, performance reviews, security procedures, order processing, communications infrastructure, identity management, financial reporting, and the like. When it comes to such systems, it is critical that they be standard, stable, and persistent. These truly are shared services, and they should be understood as public utilities where everyone abides by the same set of rules in order to ensure an efficient platform for the enterprise as a whole. That is why they should be centrally funded.

When executives from service-consuming organizations ask for exceptions to these standardized regimes, often because they have an alternative in mind that would make their organization more effective, their requests should usually be declined. Efficiency trumps effectiveness under a systems regime. Of course, if a number of similar requests build up, that is usually a signal that the system should be reengineered to better serve one and all, and the sooner, the better. Band-Aiding the problem with individual workarounds in the interim, however, is a poor alternative.

Programs, by contrast, represent a very different case. If systems lay down the tracks upon which the performance engine runs, programs provide the fuel. Promotional programs capture the attention of customers and partners; lead generation programs fill the pipeline and help shepherd the sales process; recruiting programs secure core expertise and populate the ranks; onboarding and training programs get new recruits up to speed as quickly as possible; organizational development programs get people aligned to succeed; reengineering programs extract scarce resources trapped in unproductive processes; quality programs work to keep them from getting trapped in the first place; and IT works behind the scenes to develop customized programs to support differentiated processes both inside and outside the enterprise.

Stepping back from all this activity, we see that programs are services that deliver specific outcomes to targeted groups of users at specified points in time, with priority given to the performance zone. As such they have, or should have, specific target customers funding their efforts, and in that context the focus should be on maximizing the funding organization's productivity, even when the shared-services organization itself has to take a productivity hit to do so. In other words, when it comes to programs, improving the effectiveness of the customer takes priority over maximizing the efficiency of the service provider.

To reinforce this principle, whereas systems should be funded out of a corporate budget, programs should be funded out of earmarks in the budgets of the organizations consuming their services. Operationally, budget for these programs is still managed by the service-providing function, but actual program spending needs to be authorized by the cell in the performance matrix to which it will be allocated as a controllable indirect expense and not simply incurred at the discretion of the organization providing the service. This creates two good outcomes. First, it makes the service-consuming organization accountable for its program spending, causing it to think twice about spending what otherwise appears to be a free resource ("Your tax dollars at work!"). And second, it puts the service-providing organization on notice that program work is not an entitlement but rather must be earned, potentially in competition with an external supplier.

In short, with respect to programs the intent is to set up a *market* dynamic in place of a *bureaucratic* one, thereby eliminating the practice of simply allocating the cost of shared services as an overhead expense, something that creates widespread resentment as well as devaluing the services so funded. To tee this up properly, extra time needs to be set aside during the annual planning process for performance zone executives to forecast their program demands from the various shared services functions and incorporate them into their budgets as earmarked controllable indirect expenses, and for the shared services executives to budget and allocate resources properly to meet those demands.

Managing End of Life Programs— A New Centrally Funded Shared Service

A persistent inhibitor of productivity in the performance matrix comes from hanging on to offerings with increasingly dwindling amounts of revenue even when it would be more productive to just end-of-life them. Column owners in the performance matrix are often concerned about not ruffling the feathers of a major customer, and row owners seeking to make their number are loath to forego even modest amounts of revenue, especially when they entail high gross margins as these hypermature offers often do. Unfortunately, neither of these perspectives takes into account the opportunity cost of not focusing on higher-priority efforts nor the productivity impact of maintaining underutilized SKUs, exception-laden contracts, special-services provisioning, and the like. These are not particularly worrisome issues in nondisrupted times, but when enterprises fail to free themselves from such entanglements, they are in no position to cope with the challenges of disruption.

The best way to address this issue is to establish an autonomous End of Life (EOL) shared service in the productivity zone. Think of this as a hospice organization whose sole function is to take custody of expiring offerings and manage the EOL process end to end. In terms of the Three Horizons model, this is a fourth horizon, what we have taken to calling Horizon 0. The goal is to free the company from the pull of the past, in this case specifically from the long tail of residual products that are robbing it of agility and focus.

Setting up EOL programs as a shared service requires establishing a unique set of protocols along the following lines:

- Transfer all revenues, product responsibility, resources, and expenses, including head count, from the performance matrix row owner to the Horizon 0 program owner. All subsequent actions, listed below, are performed by the EOL program manager who is the sole responsible party going forward.

- Eliminate all sales compensation from the EOL product and its related services.
- Identify all affected constituencies, alert them to impending EOL actions, and get their feedback on the impact these actions may have.
- Develop an EOL calendar that does its best to mitigate the disruption being caused but sets clear milestones and end dates that will not be revisited.
- Drive outcomes to meet planned milestones, releasing staff for reassignment on a predetermined schedule.
- Accrue any residual revenue as well as all costs of layoffs and any other shutdown expenses to the EOL program.
- Hold EOL managers accountable for keeping program cadence, meeting schedule, maintaining customer and partner relationships, and minimizing cost and any other negative impacts.

People are always saying, "We can't kill anything around here." They do not realize that expiring products are like zombies—they need a special touch. An EOL shared service is just the thing.

Governance

In most corporations the various organizations that make up the productivity zone operate relatively autonomously. This makes sense given the wide disparity of disciplines and specialized expertise that make up this zone. That said, meeting the challenge of a disruptive innovation, whether as an opportunity or a threat, requires a much more coordinated response. Resources that may be duplicated across functions are desperately needed elsewhere, and unanticipated challenges often must be met by novel integrations of previously siloed functions. All this calls for a layer of governance to span the entire zone.

One traditional solution is to have all the various leads report to a chief operating officer. This can work well when that role specifically excludes any management responsibility for the performance zone, as it did, for example, at Microsoft in the 1990s when Bob Herbold came over from P&G to play this role. Most COOs, however, seek a broader span of control, one that incorporates both the performance zone and the productivity zone. This, unfortunately, can dilute the attention the productivity zone needs while at the same time put a layer of management between the performance matrix and the CEO. That, in turn, can create ambiguity of authority at the very top of the enterprise, which, unless there is an exceptional relationship of trust between the CEO and the COO, does not bode well for anyone. It is not surprising, therefore, that the role of COO has fallen out of favor in recent times, at least in the high-tech sector.

An emerging, and in my view, far better, approach to governance in the productivity zone is to aggregate its operations into three clusters, as follows:

- Customer- and market-facing functions, typically led by a chief marketing officer,
- Supply chain- and ecosystem-facing functions, typically led by a vice-president of operations, and
- Internally facing functions, typically led by a vice-

president of finance and administration.

In nondisrupted times these three operate as an informal council coordinating activities across the zone, with a spike in their interactions during the horse-trading portion of the annual budgeting process. In times of disruption, by contrast, they must forge much closer ties, typically going to a weekly commits cadence, to drive more dramatic changes in resource reallocation. At such times it is critical that the productivity zone operate as a single team rather than a set of isolated and entitled fiefdoms, and this is only possible if there are long-standing relationships of trust among the principals running the zone.

With that thought in mind, let us turn to the kinds of resource reallocation required.

Playing Offense in the Productivity Zone

When an enterprise commits to creating a net new line of business and scaling it to material size, it puts itself under enormous resource pressure, and virtually all of its relief must come from the productivity zone. *Programs* are the primary source of this relief, and they must take precedence over systems for the foreseeable future (compliance, by contrast, remains sacrosanct—there is never any relief from paying its taxes).

At the outset the most immediate pressure is felt by the internally facing functions. HR must address urgent hiring needs, often involving out-of-band compensation packages and organizational adaptations. Business development must deliver the game-changing acquisition within the window of opportunity. Legal has to negotiate make-or-break contracts with unfamiliar terms and conditions. Investor relations has to tell a new narrative, one that will create air cover for the impending J-curve. None of these can be handled as business as usual. All need special programs to land them safely and expeditiously.

On the customer-facing side, disruptive innovation makes for hot marketing copy, so it is a time of great excitement. But there will also be a lot of gaps—new audiences to address, new narratives to invent, new media to engage, new ecosystems to enlist—and there is no time for learning on the job. CMOs have to reallocate their budgets, often dramatically, to rent the expertise for the short term, bringing the inside team up to speed as fast as possible. This is expensive, especially since you want to engage the best, and cuts will have to come from somewhere.

But here's the thing—these cuts can't come from within marketing itself. It has two megachallenges on its plate: drive the adoption of the next big thing, and support a resource-depleted performance matrix in making its numbers in the established lines of business. Resources will have to be reallocated *across* functions with cuts coming from organizations that are not directly in the line of fire. In a world of fiefdoms and silos this will inevitably be perceived as a self-serving argument, so it is critical that the council that governs the productivity zone have sufficiently established relationships of trust to do the right thing.

Finally, in the externally facing operations, the biggest challenges come from the emerging line of business playing havoc with established systems and processes. Its requirements are not only anomalous, they are subscale, and under any normal rules of engagement the business would be banned from the performance matrix and the operations that support it. But these are not normal times; they are instead a race to a tipping point, a point in the future when the outside world stops pushing back in resistance to the new paradigm and starts pulling it forward. Until that time, the operations functions have to field programs to cope with the disruption and hold their existing systems together as best they can. Effectiveness in disruption trumps efficiency in established operations—but you try telling that to an operations executive! It is because of challenges like these that the CEO has to play such an active role in the transformation zone.

Playing Defense in the Productivity Zone

When an established line of business gets disrupted, incumbent market leaders have to scramble to field a competitive response. This shifts the fulcrum of competitive advantage. What once were signature capabilities are now at best table stakes; at worst, they are actually liabilities. You need to move your troops to a new part of the battlefield and engage them in a new formation.

In this new world, you are not trying to differentiate for competitive advantage. You are trying to neutralize to catch up. You don't have the time to come up with something beyond compare. You need to get to good enough, fast enough. That is the job of the performance zone, sponsored by the transformation zone, with help from the incubation zone—an all-hands-on-deck endeavor that trumps every other priority for the foreseeable future.

All this, of course, takes time, talent, money, and management attention. Where are those resources going to come from? From out of the hide of the legacy operating model, that's where! And that is the job of the productivity zone. It must do whatever it can to optimize the current operations. The goal is to extract resources from traditional workflows to repurpose for the transformation under way. These legacy processes are deeply ingrained in the company's culture and led by well-established leaders who are used to commanding the lion's share of the annual operating budget. Now those same leaders will be asked to do a lot more with a lot less—that is, continue to grow earnings but do so with a significantly smaller head count and budget.

How do you do that? Well, it's a bit like drilling for oil. There are always trapped resources in any system struggling against the restrictions of an aging operating model, and your goal is to extract them to deploy against a new agenda. The key is to make sure you are targeting a resource-rich process, one that is consuming a lot of the kind of resources you want to be using elsewhere. This is likely to be something mission-critical, so there is real risk entailed in reengineering it. But that risk pales in comparison to the risk of not freeing up resources to accelerate the modernization of your operating model. What you must not do under any circumstances is undertake a reengineering initiative that, even when successful, does not move the needle when it comes to freeing up the scarce resources you need to redeploy. This may end up saving a bucket full of money, but that only postpones the reckoning. You need to free up talent—that's the only deliverable that really matters.

Once you have one or more talent-trapping processes

targeted, then the Six Levers model outlined below provides a framework for how best to proceed:

The Six Levers

1. *Centralize.* Having identified the process to be reengineered and socialized the idea to get support for the effort, your first step is to centralize its governance under a single individual who has both the responsibility and the authority to set new policy and enforce it, end to end. Reengineering is an unpopular act that does not lend itself to democratic decision making. To be sure, at the front end during the design phase you want to engage collaboratively to determine how best to reform the legacy process, but once that effort is under way you need to take a command-and-control approach to see it through the execution phase. Put your commander in place at the beginning, establish executive sponsorship for the person and the role, and then support the heck out of him or her whenever the inevitable rebellion surfaces. Backsliding during a reengineering effort only serves to diminish the rewards while extending the misery.

2. *Standardize.* Established enterprises typically grow through multiple mergers and acquisitions, so "standard" operating procedures end up varying substantially across equivalent functions. Such variations reduce agility, impede mobility, increase cost of maintenance, and invite errors. Talent

gets trapped just compensating for systems that do not talk to each other well. Standardizing to a single instance attacks this kind of waste while establishing a baseline from which all future changes can be launched. It can be a bit draconian, but when disruption strikes, there is no time to pussyfoot around.

3. *Modularize*. This is an act of creative imagination in which you decompose the process targeted for reengineering into its functional component elements while ignoring the organizational boundaries that govern its operation currently. Your goal is to reexamine each step in terms of how it changes the state of the workload being processed. Every desired state change deserves its own step, and every step should deliver a desired state change. Note that you are not reengineering yet. You are just putting the value-adding activity more clearly in view while simultaneously identifying as waste those procedures that do not contribute to any desirable state change. That's where the scarce resources you are seeking to liberate are trapped.

4. *Optimize*. This is the execution phase, the one where you implement the redesigned process to eliminate waste. Typically it involves merging some tasks, eliminating others, automating repetitive operations, enabling self service where appropriate, leveraging technology solutions where available, predicting and preempting bottlenecks and breakdowns, and providing an SOS button to push whenever something doesn't work. Occasionally it may involve

completely revamping the process to leverage a next-generation system that addresses the task in a completely different way. The critical goal here is not to save money nor to be more efficient, although both are likely to occur. Rather, it is to make yourself more effective by freeing up resources you need to repurpose for core. If you do not accomplish this goal, you will have wasted your time.

5. *Instrument.* There is a law of diminishing returns when it comes to optimization. At some point in your reengineering, therefore, your goal is to stabilize the process in its then-current state and run it as efficiently as possible going forward. Now is the time to instrument the process, overlaying a control system that monitors key state indicators to verify that quality is being maintained and to detect any process drift that needs attention. This frees up substantial management time for other tasks while at the same time ensuring critical oversight.

6. *Outsource.* If the process is properly instrumented and demonstrably under control, and if it cannot be automated in its entirety, it is now a candidate for outsourcing. This is worth doing if it frees up scarce resources you want to use elsewhere. Service levels are set by the process control systems you have already put in place, thereby maintaining visibility into key process parameters even as immediate oversight is being transferred to the outsourcer. You still have to monitor the systems, but you are no longer responsible for running them.

One final point: the Six Levers framework is linear by design. You cannot simply centralize (Lever 1) and then outsource (Lever 6). That results in a "your mess for less" approach that entails arbitrarily set service-level agreements, endless changes of scope, impossibly delayed adjustments, massively overrun cost estimates, and generally grief all around. You have to *earn* the right to outsource, and you do that by implementing Levers 2 through 5 to get there.

Faults and Fixes

Similar to what we saw with the performance zone, a prolonged period of market stability can allow inertia to build up around subpar practices in the productivity zone as well. The results are annoying but not mission-critical to fix. Under the pressure of category disruption, however, these faults create execution risks that must be addressed directly and swiftly. Here are some of the most common ones:

- *Failure to align with performance matrix leaders around program priorities.* This happens when a shared-services provider implementing a program disagrees with that program's customer about the nature of the program itself. It happens a lot because customers know what they want and service providers know what is best. The key fix here is to separate the *how* from the *what*. The program's customers are funding the program—that gives them the right to specify the *what*. If the program service providers cannot agree with this what, they must turn down the assignment, letting the program customers take their budget elsewhere. On the other hand, once that *what* has been agreed to, the program services providers have the right to specify the *how*. This, after all, is their field of expertise. If the program customers cannot agree with that approach, again, they need to take their work elsewhere, but only after an escalation to make sure the enterprise's budget dollars are not being wasted arbitrarily.

- *Failure to align with performance matrix leaders around system priorities.* Here the shoe is on the other foot. A system user is demanding a special accommodation, and the system owners have inappropriately acceded to it, often because they are midlevel managers unable to hold their ground against an insistent senior executive. This sets a horrible precedent, so it is critical that process owners escalate this issue to higher levels. Systems are the backbone of the enterprise. They are corporate assets. They are not to be trifled with, even by bigwigs. Top management needs to be very firm here.

- *Trying to EOL an offering while leaving it within the business unit that has traditionally sponsored it.* This just never works, for all the reasons we mentioned earlier. The correct fix is to implement the Horizon 0 approach outlined above via a dedicated shared service that operates in the productivity zone outboard of the performance matrix.

- *Majoring in minors.* This happens when productivity initiatives focus on optimizing workloads that have little impact on the core business and shy away from undertaking the real resource hogs. In high tech, this means they fail to engage with the powerhouses of engineering and sales, the two workhorses that drive enterprise value, and instead focus on, say, wasted office space. This is all very well during normal times, but when category disruption strikes, sales and engineering are ground zero for resource reallocation. That makes them the most critical functions to reengineer, even when they themselves are resisting this notion. To address this need requires performance matrix leaders to weigh in with CEO backing. The driving issue is: Where are we going to get the resources we need to meet the twin challenges of making the number and getting our next big thing to the tipping point? Your best bet is that they are trapped in legacy processes in engineering and sales and that through applying the Six Levers you can free them up.

Concluding Remarks

To sum up, best practices for managing the productivity zone include:

1. Organizing and funding operations within each shared-services function to explicitly separate the three classes of deliverables.
   - Funding *compliance* investments out of a central budget with its own reporting structure up to the CEO and the board.
   - Funding *systems* investments out of a central

budget, making sure to allocate this overhead to the CFO, not to the horizon leaders.

- Funding *program* investments out of a distributed budget controlled by the various performance matrix or function leaders and allocated back to them as a *controllable indirect expense*.

2. Managing systems centrally, and holding systems managers accountable for operational excellence based on industry benchmarks and established standards. Make clear to the rest of the enterprise that exceptions to system processes, however desirable to the exception-requesting party, are normally suboptimal for the enterprise as a whole and will not be looked on favorably.

3. Managing program management on a decentralized basis out of the program consumers' budgets, and allowing open-market dynamics to create an appropriate level of quality, efficiency, and accountability. Allow sufficient time in the annual planning process for program budget owners to engage with shared-services providers to establish the expected workloads and staffing for the coming year. Overall, lower transaction costs should favor internal service providers in providing most services, but factors of time or talent may swing the decision to an outside contractor.

4. Establishing an End of Life Horizon 0 capability reporting to the most senior supply chain executive in the productivity zone. Staff EOL programs with middle managers who have organizational longevity and know how to get things done inside

your enterprise. Provide heavyweight top executive support to these managers whenever a senior executive seeks to work around the system.

5. When under pressure from a category disruption, launching reengineering initiatives to extract resources from work that is still mission critical but no longer strategic, the goal being to redirect budget and head count in a new strategic direction. This is by nature an intensely political action that requires leadership, patience, and determination, along with an ability to engage and enlist the teams involved to set aside their parochial interests and do the right thing for the enterprise as a whole.

Overall, the perennial challenge in managing the productivity zone is to keep your teams sharp at all times. In good times it is easy to fall into lax habits. Inertia carries you along, and you can easily be lulled into thinking you are in better shape than you actually are. When disruption hits, it forces everyone to play up to an A game, and there is no time to go back and make up for prior slacking off. So *get in shape, stay in shape* is the only safe way to go.

CHAPTER FIVE
The Incubation Zone

The incubation zone is home to Horizon 3 investments, the ones that are not expected to reach material size for several years, sometimes considerably longer. This begs one question right from the start: Why should shareholder funds be allocated to such long-term efforts in the first place? Why not leave them to public funding, university research, or the venture-capital community and focus on matters closer to hand?

These are totally appropriate questions, and they serve to set a high bar for established enterprises to invest. The key criteria an offering must meet to warrant Horizon 3 investment from a publicly held corporation are:

- It embodies a disruptive innovation that can drive a *10X improvement* in a performance metric of great importance to the target market. Otherwise it simply will not have sufficient impact to drive a new category development life cycle all the way through to scale.

- It represents a business opportunity that has the potential to scale to *material size*, the minimum threshold being 10 percent of total enterprise revenue at the time when it reaches scale, to be achieved through a combination of nonlinear organic growth and acquisitions. Otherwise it will not be able to make a stable place for itself in the performance matrix.

- When successful at scale, it should represent a *net new line of business* for the enterprise, as opposed to an adjacency to an existing line of business. Only the former can trigger a step function change in the enterprise's overall market capitalization, and anything less than that reward does not compensate sufficiently for the venture risk involved.

In sum, the incubation zone represents precious real estate that should not be confused with experimentation with next-generation technologies and business models. That sort of thing can be done in a Skunk Works or a lab, a domain where learning is the prime objective and fast failure is actually a form of success. Consider these seed investments if you will. Entry into the incubation zone proper, by contrast, requires making a credible claim to becoming the next big franchise. That is what the enterprise is really looking for. That is the whole point of Horizon 3.

In such a context each funded entity is charged to develop and bring to market a disruptive innovation, one that will create or participate in an emerging category with the potential to generate billions of dollars of sales within less than a decade. In less than half that time, it is the responsibility of the funded entity not only to produce a highly competitive product but also to scale itself into a viable business, roughly between 1 and 2 percent of total corporate revenues, depending on the size of the enterprise overall. At that scale it qualifies for transitioning to the transformation zone, where the goal will be to scale it an additional order of magnitude to achieve a tipping-point threshold of roughly 10 percent of total corporate revenue. To start with a business smaller than 1 percent normally makes no sense—the journey is just too long and the object of attention is just too small.

In short, the incubation zone is a staging area for substantial businesses, a base camp within which one can scale to $100M or more in revenues (the 1 percent threshold for a $10B enterprise) without leaving the zone. Even at this stage, businesses are still too small to manage as rows in the performance matrix, their granularity acting like grit in the gears of that bigger machine. At the same time, however, they are also way too large to manage as programs or projects. They need to have specialized sales, marketing, and professional services to compete against other startups on their market-facing side, and they need customized supply chain services to design, build, and operate their next-generation disruptive offers. In sum, in the incubation zone you are not just funding R&D engineering—you're funding entire companies.

Governance

Managing an incubation zone inside an established enterprise requires innovation in its own right. The goal is to balance the best practices from venture capital with those of a publicly held corporation. That was the challenge John Chambers, CEO of Cisco Systems, gave to Marthin DeBeer in 2006 when he charged him with developing the Emerging Technology Group. Although Cisco subsequently struggled with navigating the transformation zone with these businesses, their practices in the incubation zone were world-class. Here is the model that grew out of that effort.

Managing the Incubation Zone
Venture-Style Independent Operating Units

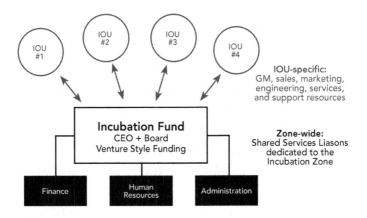

The critical elements of this model are as follows:

- Each entity in the incubation zone operates as an Independent Operating Unit (IOU) with its own general manager and dedicated resources for product development, product delivery, sales, and marketing.

Although it is not a full-fledged P&L, it should feel and act like a startup company, not an R&D project.

- The IOUs themselves are funded outboard of the annual planning calendar, based on milestone target dates that are not expected to align with the fiscal year. The overall size of the venture fund, on the other hand, is adjusted annually during the corporate planning process. Once the fund size is set, it is ring-fenced such that Horizon 3 incubation projects compete for funding with each other only, never with Horizon 1 initiatives in the productivity zone or lines of business in the performance zone.

- The incubation zone as a whole is governed by a "venture board" that determines what areas of innovation warrant investment, which business plans get funded, which IOUs get follow-on funding, what performance rewards go to which general managers, and the like. Ideally, this board comprises the head of the incubation zone, the CEO, the head of products, the head of engineering, and one or two other executives who have strong aptitudes for strategy and innovation management.

- The entire portfolio of IOUs in the incubation zone is supported by a small team of liaisons to the various shared services in the productivity zone. This team is specifically tasked with adjudicating the differences between the venture cadence of the IOU and the standard systems of the enterprise as a whole. Their charter is to keep the IOU team from getting bogged down or overwhelmed by corporate systems requirements, while at the same time maintaining viable compliance standards. This is particularly important when the IOU is initiated via an acquisition.

- Each IOU is subject to a venture-funding discipline that requires meeting specific milestones in order to secure the next round, typically along the following lines:
  - *Initial seed round:* Validate the technology.
  - *Series A round:* Build a minimum viable product and validate the market.
  - *Series B round:* Target a beachhead market, build a viable whole-product solution, and win a dominant share of new sales within that segment.
  - *Series C round:* Scale into adjacent markets in preparation for an exit into the transformation zone.
- When IOUs fail to reach a milestone, they will often warrant getting a second chance. They normally will not deserve a third. Spaces in the incubation zone are too valuable to waste. When IOUs fail to win their next round of funding, they should be disassembled immediately, with any technology wins assimilated by an existing line of business where appropriate, and the staff reassigned.

Playing Offense in the Incubation Zone

Playing offense in the incubation zone is directly comparable to running a venture-backed startup. Milestones are defined in terms of state changes in the business that warrant a step-up in valuation. Productizing the technology, winning the first major lighthouse customer, and winning dominant share in your first target market segment are the key inflection points. The first is gained through working with customers who are technology enthusiasts and actively support the beta test effort, the second with a few visionary business leaders who are willing to take a big risk to steal a march on their competition, and the third with pragmatist process owners who are in a jam and are willing to embrace your disruptive innovation if it can provide a way out. These are well-established milestones. They are truly the ones that matter. The key to winning in the incubation zone is not to get distracted by anything else.

To achieve the first milestone takes technical talent, some of which should come from in-house, else you risk pursuing a dream that does not connect back to the enterprise. That said, additional expertise should come from outside, specifically in the disruptive technology itself. Finally, even at this early stage, you need an entrepreneur, a single point of accountability for delivering the sum of all future outcomes. Remember, you are not funding a research project—you are funding a company.

To achieve the second milestone you will need to supplement the technical team with a professional services capability that can design and deliver the lighthouse customer project. The leader here needs to be exceptional—able to conceptualize the customer's challenge, master the principles of the disruptive innovation, and forge from these end points a bridge between the two, one that can operate in the real world and deliver to the customer a 10X improvement on a key performance metric. The motto for this stage of the entrepreneurial journey is, "Sell yourself into trouble, work your way out." It is not for the faint of heart.

Lighthouse customer wins put your fledgling enterprise on the map, but they do not a line of business make. That takes winning a dominant share of a target market segment, a cohort of customers who have collectively committed to the new technology as a platform for remediating some broken market-specific operating process that is putting them all in jeopardy. This is what crossing the chasm is all about: providing the whole product that solves the compelling reason to buy for a single cohort of customers sharing a common pain. Once again, the team needs to recruit outside talent to achieve this milestone. In this case the critical ingredient is domain expertise in the target segment's business process challenges, in part born from business experience working in that segment, ideally supplemented with a personal network that can accelerate introductions to target prospects. The goal is to rally the company around a solution business model that is relevant, powerful, and replicable. That is what will cause customers in the target segment to rally around the company.

When an IOU has achieved its third milestone, it has passed through a tipping point and become a going concern. That is, it is a real business with real customers with attractive growth prospects. It is still an order of magnitude subscale for participation in the performance matrix, but it is now a legitimate candidate for transitioning to the transformation zone. This is the goal of every IOU. That said, because that zone can process only one business transformation at a time, and because these transformations take two to three years to effect, only a small fraction of the portfolio will ever achieve this outcome. What about all the other IOUs?

When an IOU has not been selected for the transformation zone, it must embrace one of the following remaining alternative routes to exit:

- Assimilate into an existing line of business already established in the performance matrix, reconfiguring itself to be a sustaining innovation rather than a disruptive one. This immediately gives it the scale needed to operate in the performance zone, and it will also give the established business a much-needed midlife kicker. This is not a home run, but it is a base hit, and it does help win ball games.

- Postpone its deployment and keep its place in the incubation zone, taking the extra time to be even more ready to scale when its turn comes. This can work well if the business is nascent enough. It is likely to be a one-time-only option, however, since five years is a good rule of thumb for maximum time spent in this zone.

- Spin out the business with the help of external private capital, the parent company retaining a modest equity stake and favorable IP rights. This is not a road enterprises take very often, but they should. It frees them from the distraction of a highly compelling business, one that they will drive to ruin if they don't set it free, and it creates good will and occasionally a bonanza return for the corporation as a whole. Failing such a provision, the team often just leaves anyway.

- Sell the business to a company than can better capitalize on its opportunities. This is in effect a salvage operation that is sufficiently demanding that it should be undertaken only when the assets are large enough to be material or the M&A relationship with the buyer is already well established. Otherwise it is too much of a distraction.
- Shut the effort down.

The key point here is that space in the incubation zone is at a premium, and all startups have a sell-by date. The opportunity cost of not forcing these moves is to leave yourself saddled with a second-rate innovation portfolio to post up against an all-star lineup of competitors—not a promising position.

Playing Defense in the Incubation Zone

When a disruptive attack on the performance zone is sufficiently threatening to trigger a transformation zone response, the incubation zone must realign itself with the new priorities. Specifically, the top priority is to neutralize the disruption by modernizing the established franchise's operating model as quickly as possible. In this regard, any technology from the IOUs that can help needs to be made available immediately, regardless of its impact on the IOU.

This can be accomplished in the following way:

- The venture board reviews the current portfolio of IOU technologies with the performance matrix leaders under attack, and together they target the relevant ones.

- The GMs of the IOUs with the relevant technologies are brought into the process to determine the efficacy and feasibility of integrating their next-generation capabilities with the more mature set of offers.

- Once the desirability of a technology transfer has been determined, the IOU team must make it their number-one priority, regardless of the consequences to their own incubating business. This means revamping their existing road map and assigning the top technical talent to the new project, reporting dotted line into the performance matrix row leader under attack for the duration of the effort.

Finally, if the consequence of this abrupt change in direction is to derail the IOU for good, everyone has to take this in stride. This was not the end that anyone had envisioned, but disruption creates collateral damage. There is no getting around it.

Faults and Fixes

As you can see from all of the above, this approach to funding and managing disruptive innovation is not standard corporate operating procedure. But that in effect is my point. Established enterprises have earned the reputation of not being able to innovate. Interestingly, that is not actually the case. They can and do innovate. What they cannot do is bring those innovations to scale. This is due to mismanagement in two zones, the incubation zone and the transformation zone. We will address the latter in the following chapter.

For now, let us make sure we address the following mistakes specific to the incubation zone:

- *Separating technology development from market development.* The former is typically done in a corporate laboratory or the like, the goal being to transfer a prototype product to a divisional sponsor to take it to market. This never works. The product is too immature and the market too undeveloped to reward the investments an established division would have to make to bring it to material size. The thing just gets lost in the shuffle, eventually getting tacked onto an established product line as an accessory. If you have a corporate lab, it needs to be treated as a feeder mechanism to the incubation zone, not a substitute for it.

- *Sharing resources between IOUs and the performance matrix.* Typically, enterprises try to leverage their scaled go-to-market capabilities in sales, marketing, and professional services to enable and support the scaling of a promising incubating business. Initially this can result in some serendipitous successes, but eventually the incubated entity finds itself playing second fiddle to established lines of business, especially when the latter are under significant pressure to make their number. Thus, at a time when the IOU needs an exceptionally responsive go-to-market capability, either to execute a pivot in its strategy or to outperform a direct competitor, it loses its agility and falters.

- *Burdening the incubating business with the enterprise's*

obligations. Incubation is messy, and this can result in mistakes that reflect badly on a corporate brand. The temptation therefore is to require any startup carrying "our" brand to meet expectations appropriate for more established lines of business. This is simply too big a burden to bear. Instead, the executive team must provide air cover for its incubating efforts while at the same time making sure these IOUs are restricting their operations to appropriately early-adopting customers. One tactic to consider here is to create a subbrand specifically dedicated to sponsoring next-generation innovations, as Red Hat has done with its Fedora brand, underscoring the message that these are experimental ventures targeted at early adopters and are not subject to the same stringent standards as mainstream product lines.

- *Assigning the wrong type of leader.* IOUs in the incubation zone must be led by entrepreneurial GMs. A good pool to draw from is ex-CEOs from acquired companies that have successfully navigated a venture trajectory in the past. Unless you find something pretty interesting for these folks to do, they won't stick around anyway. By contrast, longtime career executives, even those with excellent track records, are not used to rolling up their sleeves to do whatever job needs doing, nor typically are they willing to push the system hard enough to get things done in a disruptive context.

- *Failing to shut down unqualified projects.* Investing in disruptive innovation is a Darwinian exercise.

It should be hard to get funded and hard to stay funded. Failure to cull the herd diffuses focus, wastes resources, and drags the entire portfolio down.
- *Funding Horizon 3 investments via the annual operating plan.* The annual budgeting process is organized around Horizon 1 lines of business. Disruptive innovations should never be competing with them for funding. Moreover, IOUs need to be funded based on milestones, not an annual planning calendar. Too many underperforming ventures get to coast for too many quarters if you only review funding decisions once a year. What can and should be adjusted each year is the overall size of the venture fund itself, with the clear understanding that access to it is restricted solely to qualified Horizon 3 opportunities.
- *Letting the performance matrix incubate Horizon 3 initiatives under the covers.* Such efforts will never scale successfully to disrupt the status quo. Their sole successful outcome is next-generation innovation within the established categories served. As already noted, this is a Horizon 1 responsibility and should not be misconstrued as Horizon 3, even when its gestation period requires several years.

Concluding Remarks

The key takeaway overall is that openings in the incubation zone should be treated as a scarce resource and not wasted on second-tier opportunities or teams. Particularly when a sector is undergoing widespread disruption, the cost of missing the next wave can be catastrophic. The enterprise simply cannot afford to back anything but A players playing in A games.

CHAPTER SIX
The Transformation Zone

The transformation zone is the mechanism by which an enterprise can free its future from the pull of the past. Initiatives here focus on responding to an emerging wave of secular growth arising out of category disruption. When the disrupted category is adjacent to the core business, established corporations can play offense. When it is their own category that is getting disrupted, they must play defense. Either way, the goal is to undertake a transformational initiative to put the enterprise on a new trajectory, one significantly different from the current one.

This gives rise to the Horizon 2 dilemma. To effectively engage with the new wave, the enterprise must reallocate substantial resources to endeavors that dramatically underdeliver on Horizon 1 performance metrics. Worse, they must extract the bulk of these resources from the existing performance matrix, putting even more pressure on

Horizon 1. Further complicating the challenge, every system in their company has evolved to reinforce the interests of the performance zone, not contravene them. The end result is that there is enormous inertial momentum around the current operations. This is a very good thing in normal times, allowing the company to generate attractive returns at low risk—indeed, the whole point of any new growth strategy is to someday achieve this state and sustain it for as long as possible.

But all that goes out the window when disruption strikes. Now staying the course is a path to going over the falls. To have a meaningful role in the new order, the enterprise will have to change its course and speed. The captain must take the helm. Leading this kind of transformation is the defining element in the CEO role, the one that sets it apart from the COO role. It is not something to undertake lightly or frequently, but when it must be undertaken, it trumps all other priorities.

Governance

Unlike the other three zones, the transformation zone is a transitory institution. It comes into existence to meet (or create) a crisis, and it passes out of existence once the crisis is resolved. Thus there is no independent, persistent body of governance. Instead, it organizes around the CEO's executive staff and co-opts that group's regular meeting cadence by claiming top priority on every agenda.

The role of the CEO itself changes dramatically in a time of disruptive innovation. During an era of sustaining innovation, the CEO is the most senior manager on the executive team, and the focus of executive activity is on good management. In an era of disruption, by contrast, CEOs must transfer the burden of managing the existing lines of business onto the rest of the executive team, with or without the help of a COO, and focus their own energies on leading the enterprise through a period of destabilizing change. In other words, sustaining initiatives demand good management; disruptive ones, extraordinary leadership.

Playing Offense in the Transformation Zone

The goal of zone offense is to leverage nonlinear growth from a category disruption to create a net new business of material size in the enterprise portfolio. To initiate this move, one takes an independent business unit from the incubation zone and repositions it as a line of business in the performance matrix, as illustrated in the following diagram:

Transformation Zone
Transformational Initiatives

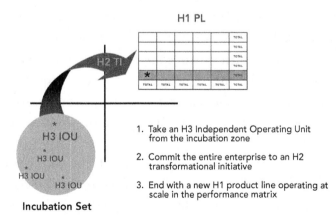

H1 PL

1. Take an H3 Independent Operating Unit from the incubation zone

2. Commit the entire enterprise to an H2 transformational initiative

3. End with a new H1 product line operating at scale in the performance matrix

Incubation Set

The CEO's first task here is to pick one—and only one—business to scale. As we have said repeatedly, allowing two or more entities into the transformation zone at the same time is a showstopper.

The CEO's second task is to sponsor a dramatic reallocation of resources, one that will put everyone's nose out of joint. That is, even though the disruptive business at present is an order of magnitude subscale, the GM of the IOU is nonetheless promoted to become a new row owner in the performance matrix. At the same time, all of the sales-focused column owners in the performance matrix are charged to deliver nonlinear growth against this new row even though the sales motion is less efficient than in the other, established lines of business. Moreover, the professional-services organization is charged to prioritize this row's projects above all others, even though they are likely to be resource-intensive, unprofitable, and a bear to manage. Finally, to complete the arc of nonlinear growth, business development is charged to find one or more at-scale acquisitions that will be personally endorsed by the GM and shepherded through the M&A process by the CEO in light of the fact that their valuation multiples will be ludicrously high when compared with the acquiring enterprise. With the onboarding of these acquisitions, scaling commences in earnest, and the period from then on until the tipping point will be one of great sacrifice and stress.

Once that tipping point is reached, the organization can restabilize. The various line functions that previously took direction from the GM under the IOU model will now migrate into and integrate with the performance zone or productivity zone function that provides their service, and take their future direction from the appropriate line function manager. The business itself will have become a material row in the performance matrix and a high-growth provider as well. The goal now is to grow inertial momentum around the new position, something the performance matrix is inherently good at.

Prior to reaching that point, however, there are deep challenges to overcome. As we discussed earlier, these include:

- *Scarce Domain Expertise.* Knowledge critical to winning sales in the new category is concentrated in the IOU sales team and virtually absent in the global sales force at large. There is a straightforward fix for this problem—implementing an overlay sales force model—but that leads to the next challenge.

- *Out-of-Band Expense-to-Bookings Ratio.* Overlay sales forces become victims of their own success, being expensive to deploy and becoming more so as they scale. Well before the materiality metric has been achieved, they will have a visibly negative impact on the operating margins of the enterprise as a whole. This normally causes the CFO to clamp down. But to cut back at this time is simply fatal: when the overlay layer is decommissioned before revenues reach the tipping point, sales momentum goes sideways, the initiative falters, and no new row appears in the performance matrix.

- *Misaligned Compensation.* Sales compensation is normally awarded for bookings productivity. Selling in Horizon 2, however, is inherently less productive than selling in Horizon 1 because first one must engage senior executives at the target customer to create budget, and then with the function managers to win the right to consume it. This fundamentally less-productive selling motion deters conventionally compensated members of the global sales team from engaging more actively with the transformational initiatives, diminishing their efforts just when they need to be maximized.

- *Account Management Resistance.* Misalignment surfaces here as well. Typically the incumbent account manager does not have a relationship with the new target customer who is often in a separate organization and who may be competing for budget with the existing customer's organization. Meanwhile, sales cycles with the traditional customer can be disrupted by the new offer, causing delays and even outright losses.

None of these problems is insoluble, but all require substantial investments of time, talent, and management attention. That is why the CEO has to make the transformational initiative the first topic on the agenda at virtually every executive staff meeting. The focus of these sessions is on acceleration. Transformational initiatives are extremely risky and exceptionally painful, so the sooner they are completed the better. The operative question for every meeting, therefore, directed by the CEO to the GM of the emerging line of business, is: "What can any of us do right now to further accelerate your progress?"

Here are some of the levers the CEO and e-staff can and should pull:

- Make the new business the headline in corporate marketing and communications messaging.
- Double sales coverage in one or two vertical markets where the new line of business has particularly compelling use cases and is getting better-than-average traction.
- Grant special terms for contracts that get marquee customers over the line.
- Add professional-services capacity to accelerate customer implementation of the disruptive offering.
- Fund additional engineering capacity to accelerate the build-out of the "me-too" feature set that complements a highly differentiated core.
- Support special deals for supply chain partners to expedite their contributions to the offering.
- Grant special retention agreements for executives from the growth acceleration acquisition to ensure they double down to support this effort.

In parallel with these special dispensations, transformation zone initiatives also demand significant sacrifices from the other three operating zones, each of which has its own inertial momentum that will resist such changes. Specifically, here's what is being asked of each:

- *Performance Zone.* Column owners in the performance matrix need to allocate up to 10 percent of their total go-to-market capacity to the transformational initiative while still achieving the metrics of the rest of the operating plan. Product row owners do not have to pay this big a tax directly—although they typically do have to curtail their hiring—but less sales capacity puts pressure on their numbers as well. In short, a single transformational initiative can and normally does consume all the contingency resources in the system and puts every cell in the performance matrix at risk.

- *Productivity Zone.* Leaders of shared-services functions need to find ways to reengineer, outsource, automate, or otherwise offload their existing workloads in order to free up program resources to help power the transformational change. This will likely include running a Six Levers project to extract resources trapped in legacy processes and could also include accelerating one or more EOL efforts. At the same time, they must continue to maintain the enterprise's underlying systems to ensure compliance, quality, and reliability. It's a bit of a "change the tires while the vehicle is still in motion" exercise, but it can't be helped. The performance matrix cannot deliver on both its operational and its transformational commitments without a significant productivity boost.

- *Incubation Zone.* GMs from the remaining IOUs in the incubation zone cannot expect access to the transformation zone for the foreseeable future. In that context, each IOU must reevaluate its own exit strategy, choosing either to wait out the current initiative for the chance to be next in line or to reconfigure itself for one of the alternative exits mentioned in the prior chapter.

These are extraordinary requests that land across the entirety of the executive team, and unless they are managed with precision and grace, they can easily become showstoppers.

To secure this kind of alignment, the CEO, with the support of the board of directors, should revamp the executive compensation plan to give everyone on the team a significant stake in the transformational initiative's success and a correspondingly painful consequence if it fails. If half of everyone's annual bonus for the next two to three years depends on the success of this one venture, it will definitely get the attention and support it needs. Indeed, the great irony is that when everyone in the enterprise actually does row in the same direction, it is actually almost impossible *not* to succeed. Established enterprises have amazing throwweight if they can coordinate it properly. The challenge is to ensure that compensation and management systems are appropriately modified to achieve precisely this kind of alignment.

One additional constituency you need to get aligned with the transformational initiative is your investor base. It is critical to prepare them for the upcoming changes before they impact the financial results and to control the ongoing narrative through which they are interpreted. You really are managing for shareholder value here, but because you are moving the fulcrum of value creation from steadily improving earnings to catching a new wave of growth, there is a nasty patch to go through before you can trumpet any success.

In this context your communication effort can be divided into three acts, as follows:

- *Act One* occurs before the new business has reached material size. Using the announcement of a major deal signed with a marquee customer, you call attention to the emerging category and the technology disruption that is driving it. Most of this narrative is about the impact the new paradigm can have in addressing important unmet needs and the early formation of an ecosystem of partners who will bring this value to market. There is no real financial news here; you are just giving the investment community a heads-up.

- *Act Two* is the one that does the heavy lifting. You must not hope to skate through a transformational initiative keeping your traditional performance numbers intact. That would take a miracle. But explanations as to why they are failing, no matter how compelling, will not head off investor angst. So you need to step up and make clear what you are up to and what people can expect for the next six to eight quarters. If you can time this with a major acquisition in the targeted category that resets the performance bar altogether, so much the better. Such an acquisition not only helps you achieve the material scale you need; it also buys you a grace period to put the new house in order, by the end of which you expect to show revenue performance metrics that growth investors can get excited about.

- *Act Three* represents the victory lap. The tipping point has been reached and passed. For the first time you will break out the financials for the new row in your performance matrix, allowing investors and analysts to revalue the company based on an additional earnings engine in a potentially uncorrelated category. Now it is critical *not* to keep things under wraps. Blending performance metrics from growth and value businesses is never a good idea—the sooner you can show each separately, the better for both.

The overall message here is that during a period of disruption, the numbers are not your friends, and you must not allow your corporate narrative to be dominated by operating ratios of any kind. Yes, those numbers will get calculated, and yes, you must be accountable to them, but they cannot be your story. That must be framed by a narrative of secular growth, a road map to a brighter future. Spreadsheets make lousy maps.

Playing Defense in the Transformation Zone

As challenging as it is to play offense in the transformation zone, it is even more difficult to play defense. Here's why.

A company earns its keep by helping its customers release trapped value in their operations. But what if the value is being trapped by your own company's offers? That is, what if the value you are delivering no longer warrants the profit margins you are extracting? It happens all the time as categories mature. It's why disruptors target established franchises. Now what?

The first thing you must realize is that in cases like this your investors' immediate interests are no longer aligned with your customers'. This is not a sustainable situation. The trapped value in your legacy model is going to get released one way or another. Customers have seen that there is a better way. Margins will deflate. Investors will be disappointed. There is no getting around it. Your only viable option now is to realign with your customer base by migrating your offers and your relationships onto a better footing.

In this context, your differentiating value proposition will be *evolution, not revolution.* In this context, the strategy for playing defense in the transformation zone is built around a three-step program: *1. Neutralize. 2. Optimize. 3. Differentiate.*

The order is critical. Organizations that succumb to a disruptive challenger make one of two mistakes. Some continue with business as usual, denying or downplaying the disruption at first, and then as their market position erodes to the point where it can no longer be ignored, they launch a series of downsizing initiatives to rationalize their businesses through optimization. All they succeed in doing is convincing everyone that they just don't get it. Alternatively, others panic and race to out-differentiate the disruptor, launching one or more half-baked incubation initiatives prematurely, meanwhile leaving their legacy in-market offerings unchanged. All this succeeds in doing is convincing everyone that they lack the mojo to win in the new market.

The winning response to disruption, by contrast, is as follows:

1. *Neutralize first.* Your first objective must be to blunt the disruptor's attack. You do this by co-opting their most visible and attractive features and bolting them on, as best you can, to your current offerings,

changing your operating model to accommodate these changes. It's a kludge, to be sure, but the goal is to get to *good enough, fast enough*, any way you can.

For example, at the time of this writing, to respond to the disruption of Uber, several San Francisco cab companies are adopting Flywheel, a mobile app that lets you summon one of their cabs, track your ride, and pay by phone. You don't rate the driver, and they haven't changed their business model to match Uber's. On the other hand, they have modernized their offering and updated their operating model in order to blunt Uber's appeal by co-opting one of its most attractive and visible features. This puts them back in the game. If you fail to neutralize, you leave the playing field to the other team. That's why "neutralize first" has to be your top priority.

2. *Optimize second.* Given the new value proposition in the market and your inability in the short term to match it, you have little choice but to reduce your prices. To do so and maintain a viable operating margin you are going to have to take cost out of your infrastructure model. Here is where the productivity zone needs to weigh in with its expertise in Six Sigma and the Six Levers. You have to act quickly, and the decisions you must make, while not difficult, are certainly not pleasant. In this context, the CEO needs to be both an active sponsor and a vigilant inspector, making sure the hard choices get made and get executed in a timely manner.

3. *Differentiate third.* This takes longer, often a lot longer. Having used neutralization to refurbish your

operating model and used optimization to revamp your infrastructure model, you have bought yourself time—actually, quite a lot of time. Now, to stake out a sustainable position for the long term, you have to use differentiation to revitalize your business model. Your legacy business model is a sitting duck. It has been in the market forever, it is still a source of trapped value, and competitors know exactly how to attack it. You must reinvent yourself for a new world.

The key to such reinvention is to reaffirm your legacy value proposition even as you revolutionize the way you fulfill it. Remember, you are the incumbent. If you can realign your firm with your customers' future needs and interests, they would prefer to stick with you. And you have time. You don't have to rip and replace the old business model. There are actually plenty of customers who want to stay with your old model for a while longer. But you do have to engineer a steady evolution to the new one, and you have to make clear from the outset where that evolution is headed.

This is what Lou Gerstner did so well at IBM. When he took the helm, the mainframe model was not dead, but it was clearly dying. Nonetheless, a lot of people still wanted to stay on it, but they needed to see a different future. IBM's legacy value proposition had always been to deliver enterprise productivity through information systems. Gerstner did not change this. But he did change IBM's business model to rotate away from hardware to software and services. And that in turn gave IBM two very successful decades. Now it is time for the company to change again—never an easy thing— but at least it has a history of having been able to do so before.

Faults and Fixes

When CEOs falter in leading a transformational initiative, here are the most common mistakes they make:

- *Undertaking two or more transformations at the same time.* This is a mistake on offense. It happens most often when two or more businesses in the incubation zone are needing to scale at the same time. Both are allowed to proceed because executive teams, well aware of the odds against any particular transformation succeeding, do not want to put all their eggs in one basket, and no CEO wants to disappoint EVPs who are deeply committed to their next big thing. Regardless of motive, given the exceptional demands even one initiative makes on the rest of the enterprise, executing two or more at the same time is simply not possible, and the consequence is certain failure.
- *Delegating the task when playing offense.* Transformations focused on adding a net new row to the performance matrix alter the very structure of the enterprise. By reason of the size of the effort, the breadth of involvement required, and the risk of the undertaking, only the CEO can sponsor these efforts. Indeed,

transformation is the signature accomplishment of a CEO's tenure and should take precedence over all other tasks. To delegate this responsibility to anyone else implies that the system as a whole should be able to absorb a transformation as business as usual. If that were true, this playbook would not have needed to be written.

- *Delegating the task when playing defense.* Here the challenge is to fend off an attack on the performance zone by coordinating a complex transformational response across all three of the other zones—the incubation zone to supply the technology to support the neutralization effort, the productivity zone to support the optimization effort, and the transformation zone to support the differentiation effort. The whole company must be interdependently engaged, and no one other than the CEO can control all these reins at the same time. If you leave the ball in the performance zone's court, its only option is to optimize, and thus begins your long, slow decline into obscurity.

- *Trying to play offense and defense in the transformation zone at the same time.* You cannot simultaneously play both the disruptor and the disruptee roles. Or, to put it another way, you cannot disrupt your way out of a disrupted category. It simply puts too much stress on both the company and the partner ecosystem. When both roles are called for, you must elect to play defense first, get your house in order, and then go on offense.

- *Competing priorities.* There are always competing priorities, many of which are truly compelling. But transformations can never be put on hold. Time is always the scarcest resource, followed by talent and management attention. The transformational initiative must be first in line for all three.
- *Incomplete alignment at the executive level.* In this scenario one or more senior executives simply choose not to suit up, preferring instead to direct their energies toward efforts more specific to their own interests. This creates just enough contention for scarce reserves to cause the effort to fail, not to mention occasioning the passive-aggressive response, "I told you so." Such lack of alignment must be rooted out early and eliminated swiftly and utterly.

Concluding Remarks

The transformation zone is the CEO zone. On offense, there is the opportunity to springboard the enterprise into a whole new dimension, the way cloud computing has reset the trajectory for Amazon, the way that music and smartphones reset it for Apple, the way that Pixar reset it for Disney, the way *The Sopranos* reset it for HBO, the way the Prius did for Toyota. On defense, there is the opportunity to reposition the franchise to give it a new lease on life, the way committing to wireless helped to reposition Verizon, the way committing to software as a service helped to reposition Adobe, the way acquiring TurboTax helped to reposition Intuit, the way acquiring WebLogic helped to reposition

BEA, the way committing to web content management helped to reposition Documentum.

Twenty years after the publication of *The Innovator's Dilemma*, we must recognize that these results are still not the norm, but frankly, it is time to stop lamenting that fact and do something about it. That is the job of the transformation zone. To succeed here, CEOs must embrace a handful of principles that run counter to conventional wisdom. Let us close this chapter by reminding ourselves of what they are:

1. *It is more important to complete the transformation than to make the number.* When your business portfolio is undisrupted and your company power intact, performance can and should be the top priority. But when both have been destabilized, either by you betting big to enter a new category or some other company betting big to take one of yours away, your entire future is at risk, and you must make securing it your number-one objective. That means transformation takes precedence.

2. *When you undertake two transformations at the same time, it is impossible to succeed with either.* There is no such thing as two top priorities. There can only be one. And when just one has the power to capsize your entire operation all by itself, it is folly to consider adding a second. You are not reducing risk—you are guaranteeing failure.

3. *To complete a transformation, every leader and function must make its success their top priority—period!* This is a matter of cadence and alignment. If anyone in the boat is rowing the wrong way at the wrong time, it

throws the entire operation off. When that person is a leader, it signals to the troops that alignment is not mandatory. In times of disruption, alignment is mandatory. No exceptions.

If you can secure these three principles, your next transformation should succeed.

CHAPTER SEVEN

Installing Zone Management

When it comes to installing anything new, as golf instructors tell their pupils everywhere, it is all in the setup. In this short chapter we will outline a series of steps to take during the annual planning process to get your enterprise zoned to win.

1. *Zone your orgs.* Every organization as well as every major initiative needs to be funded out of one—and only one—zone. That choice of zone defines the contract between the entity and the enterprise in terms of one of four paradigms—performance, productivity, incubation, or transformation. There must be no confusion as to which contract model is being applied. Choose one.

   That said, once an organization has been funded, its leader is free to deploy the funding received in whatever manner best serves. That is, leaders can create a four zones model inside their own domains as a way of setting up internal contracts with team members inside their function. For example, while most of the people on my team might be focused on delivering, say, a performance objective, I might choose to have some working to incubate a future option and others developing a productivity tool for the rest to use. All of that is my choice as manager of the function. What I do not have permission to do is expose this complexity to the rest of the enterprise. From its point of view, my organization operates within a single zone and according to the protocols of that zone.

2. *Lock in the performance matrix.* It is important to clarify and formalize the structure of the performance matrix right from the start. This is the foundation of every established enterprise. Each of its rows represents a major source of bookings and revenues greater than 10 percent of the total. Similarly, each of its columns represents a sales channel accountable for greater than 10 percent of that same total. Each row and column has a unique owner who is responsible for its subtotals. The sum of all the row subtotals rolls up to the head of product, the sum of all the column subtotals to the head of sales. The grand total is owned by the CEO and the CFO.

The budget process begins with the CEO, the CFO, and the heads of product and sales. They publish a pro forma performance matrix with the grand total and all the various subtotals already set.

The row and column owners then meet collectively to allocate these targets to each of the various cells in the matrix. From these targets matrix leaders determine the resources they will need to meet them, in terms of head count, direct operating expenses, and controllable indirect expenses in the form of supporting programs.

At this point there will typically be considerable gaps between the "bid" for resources from the matrix leaders and the "ask" of the senior executives to constrain them. These gaps can be closed by adding more resources in the performance zone, funding more programs in the productivity zone, renegotiating financial targets, or finding more creative approaches to making the existing targets within the existing constraints. Needless to say, there is a lot of horse trading that goes on at this point, no different from any other annual planning process. But here is the difference when it comes to zone management: when the horse trading is done and the dust settles, the final commitments and allocations are directly reflected in the contents of each and every cell in the performance matrix, and they have been explicitly endorsed and cosponsored by the joint row and column owners responsible for each cell.

The power of this outcome must not be underestimated. Not only have the direct accountabilities been established in the performance zone but the indirect programs needed to achieve those outcomes have also been explicitly identified and funded as controllable indirect expenses. The result is a simple chart that can serve as a red/yellow/ green dashboard to guide each of the quarterly business reviews for the upcoming year, not to mention also serving as the basis for performance compensation systems. The more ambiguity you can drive out of the plan via this process, the tighter your ship will run.

3. *Activate the productivity zone.* All cost centers must continually fight the battle of the bulge, and the annual planning process is the place to start. This is where zero-based budgeting makes sense. The first order of business is to establish a set of organizational units such that all indirect spending rolls up to a manageable number of accountable executives. Within this construct each unit should identify the programs it intends to conduct on behalf of other organizations and negotiate the deliverables and funding required with the program sponsors in those organizations. In this way, the power of the purse for controllable indirect expenses is put in the hands of the program consumers while at the same time crediting the program-supplying organization with an expense offset.

Once the program funding has been sorted out, everything else is corporate overhead. Some of this will go to compliance obligations, but the bulk will go to building and maintaining enterprise systems. Here again the bulge must be fought. It should be an annual goal to apply Six Sigma and Six Levers principles to reengineer corporate systems to make them both more efficient and more effective. This is the one time when productivity program dollars can actually be spent inside the productivity zone. The goal is to do more with less, by leveraging technology, experience, and innovation. Doing more with less is a readily achievable goal provided you explicitly charter programs to accomplish this outcome. It's when you just cut budget and hope for the best that you get into trouble. Worse, when you simply declare a uniform percentage cut across all budgets regardless, you have abdicated your leadership role altogether.

4. *Fence off the incubation zone.* The annual planning process is *not* the time to get into the specifics of funding independent operating units within the incubation zone. That process follows a venture cadence based on milestones, not calendars. What should be established at this time, on the other hand, is the size of the incubation zone fund and the composition of the venture board that will have governance over it. Both decisions should be made by the CEO and CFO in consultation with the rest of the executive staff. Once these are set, all further incubation zone planning should happen offline.

5. *Determine the status of the transformation zone and proceed accordingly.* Annual planning processes are typically kicked off with a strategy discussion. Usually these focus on Horizon 3 and, frankly, are most often a waste of time. Horizon 3 is the purview of the venture board governing the incubation zone and not the executive staff at large. By contrast, discussions

focused on Horizon 2 are incredibly germane, and the assembled executive team is precisely the group that needs to have them.

The upshot of these discussions is to establish the status of the transformation zone for the coming year as either *inactive* (no disruption to be engaged with at present), *proactive* (playing offense to catch the next wave), or *reactive* (playing defense to prevent the next wave from catching you). Depending on which state is declared, the remainder of the planning process unfolds very differently. It is imperative, therefore, to declare one—and only one—of these states unequivocally.

Here's how the process plays out from there:

- *Inactive.* If there is no transformation under way or to be undertaken, then simply iterate the performance zone and productivity zone processes to closure. Don't let all the talk about returns from disruptive innovation fool you. Proceeding in an undisrupted state is by far the most productive way to generate attractive earnings.
- *Proactive.* To organize and play offense in the transformation zone effectively, the key steps are:
  - Add a new row to the performance matrix, representing a net new line of business to be scaled to material size, and promote the GM of that business to the status of row owner.
  - Set the pro forma numbers for each cell in the new row. These should be dictated top-down by the CEO.

- Determine the head count, operating expenses, and controllable indirect program expenses needed for the new row to make its pro forma numbers.
- Commit to this investment, and ring-fence it to hold it constant.
- Iterate the rest of the performance matrix to closure.
- In light of the above, iterate the productivity zone plan to closure.
- Reduce the funding for the incubation zone to force one or more additional exits.

- *Reactive.* To play defense in the transformation zone effectively, the key steps to follow are:
  - Identify which row or rows in the performance matrix are being directly disrupted, and erase the numbers in their cells.
  - Determine the neutralization objectives for the targeted businesses and set an aggressive date for their initial market launch.
  - Resource the neutralization effort in terms of staffing, operating expenses, and controllable indirect support programs designed to accelerate time to market. Ring-fence these resources.
  - In light of the above, reset the performance metrics for the targeted row or rows.
  - Holding those metrics constant, iterate to closure first on the rest of the performance matrix, then on the productivity zone.
  - Reduce the funding for the incubation zone.

Concluding Remarks

The intent of this chapter has been to distill the playbook down to its most prescriptive form to produce a brutally clear plan. Such a plan is a precious thing in an ever-changing world, a way to align the many in service to a single goal as well as a way to keep tabs on progress toward that goal. We all need a plan, and frameworks like this one are intended to provide the foundations needed to make one.

To put the value of this kind of planning in perspective, and to bring this book to a close, let us now turn to look at how two great companies that have engaged with the four zones framework in recent years, Salesforce and Microsoft. The former is playing offense, the latter defense.

CHAPTER EIGHT

Zoning to Win at Salesforce and Microsoft

The prescriptions outlined in the preceding chapters present zone management in an idealized form. They have emerged from a handful of client engagements conducted over the past several years, the two most impactful being with Salesforce, sponsored by Marc Benioff, CEO, and Microsoft, sponsored by Qi Lu, the executive vice-president who heads up the Applications and Services Group that includes Office, SharePoint, and Outlook, among other properties, with strong support from Satya Nadella, CEO. Each enterprise is adopting these methods in its own way, Salesforce playing the role of disruptor, Microsoft, the disruptee. Together they make bookend case examples for everything we have been talking about to this point. Let's see what each can teach us about how to zone to win.

Playing Zone Offense: The Example of Salesforce

In the spring of 2013 I had a chance to reconnect with Marc Benioff in conjunction with writing a third revision to *Crossing the Chasm*. It needed a whole new set of examples from the twenty-first century, and I could think of none better than Salesforce. After we had that discussion, he asked me what I was working on lately, and I told him about my latest book, *Escape Velocity*, which had the subtitle *Free Your Company's Future from the Pull of the Past*. Marc said he thought that might apply to Salesforce, but I was skeptical. The book was really about much older companies that had settled down into established market positions and now needed to catch their next wave or be overtaken by one crashing over them. That was not Salesforce.

Nonetheless, Marc said Salesforce had its issues, and after some discussion, I agreed to interview his direct reports and give a chalk talk at his next staff meeting. Well, the interview list grew a bit, and then a bit more, and I ended up interviewing thirty-eight people, including three board members, and two outside advisors from McKinsey and Accenture, respectively. And what was going to be a chalk talk at the next staff meeting turned out to be a full-on presentation at the next executive offsite. That presentation was well received and has subsequently resulted in me working with the team over these subsequent two years. What follows are some of the highlights of that relationship.

Initial State

"At Salesforce we do not grow and plateau—we are always high growth," was the way one person put it. Another said, "We are kind of a mix between a startup and a large successful company, and we are still learning how to control the combo." This is what we like to call a high-class problem. But a problem it was nonetheless. Here's how it looked through the lenses of the four zones:

- *Performance Zone.* There was a performance matrix of sorts, functioning best at the intersection of Sales Cloud and Service Cloud meeting the Commercial Business Unit (CBU) sales channel. But even here the row owners for the two clouds were in matrix hell, not heaven. One row owner estimated that it took twenty-seven different agreements to get anything done end to end. People called it the "daisy chain," and the only way to navigate was to follow this advice from a long-term veteran: "The way to get things done here is to find the person who owns it directly. Not on any org chart anywhere. I have a personal network. I know who to go to in order to ask the right question."

  In the case of the performance zone, all the development resources reported into engineering, all the marketing into marketing, and the row owners had product managers and not much else. Such a structure can actually work if the row owners have power of the purse—that's how Microsoft does it—but at Salesforce they did not. That meant that staffing commitments could be redirected for any number of reasons, with the row owner left holding the bag.

And the column owners weren't much better off, particularly if they were out in the regions. Sales, professional services, customer support, field marketing, and sales engineering all reported up functionally. As one very senior regional sales executive explained, "We don't work well across functions or business units. Everything is siloed and quota driven. I cannot decide anything—I am more of a sales manager than a GM." That all said, revenue that year was up 33 percent, which suggests that the company was doing some things right!

- *Productivity Zone.* This zone was overwhelmed by the challenges of continuous high growth combined with a programs-to-systems ratio that was wildly overrotated to programs. With respect to programs, marketing was trying to get a grip on things by reorganizing around an agency model at a time when sales needed better lead generation systems for pipeline coverage. Technical operations kept control on things by gating all changes to the platform through its own ranks, but that made life tough on any product team looking for fast cycle time. Data centers were managed to custom standards that needed expert attention, something that was not going to scale easily or cost effectively. HR was onboarding people in record numbers and realizing that the company's charisma—a very real asset—did not extend well beyond San Francisco.

Everywhere there was a need for systems, systems, systems, which was being met (with only marginal success) by programs, programs, programs. (The one great exception to this was Dreamforce itself, which you would think is the world's largest program on steroids, but in fact is an amazing system that delivers outstanding results year after year.)

- *Incubation Zone.* Here things were a bit chaotic, but largely in ways one would expect. The big concern was that there were a lot of little things cooking that did not look like they would scale. And there was a lot of flak from executives in the performance zone about how much of the available resources these fledgling efforts were getting while their load-bearing efforts got by with much less. It was a classic innovator's dilemma problem put best by a technical executive who said, "We are pretty good at letting acquisitions run independently at the start, but then we either integrate them into the core too soon or we let them languish and underperform their potential." (If that doesn't sound familiar to you by now, you have been reading some other book.)

The immediate problem was that all these acquisitions were at one point heralded as the next big thing, and once it became clear that they were not, it was not obvious what to do with them. There was no governance vehicle for making these calls other than appealing to Marc himself. It was pretty clear that things needed to get rationalized, and even reasonably clear on what terms, but there was no way to get it done.

There was also an underlying problem of cycle-time mismatch. All the new entrepreneurial organizations wanted to go to a very short release cycle—say, every week or two—but enterprise customers cannot abide that. Salesforce was releasing its major clouds every four months, which is unheard-of velocity in enterprise software but was way too slow for incubation. Again, as long as they could operate independently, each group could live and let live, but the whole purpose of the exercise was to integrate eventually, and there was neither a system nor a program for how that would get done.

- *Transformation Zone.* Ironically, this was the zone that worked best. Marc drives transformations. He is simply world-class at doing so. He has the charm and charisma to get people to sign up to do the impossible, and he has the market instincts and technical savvy to pick the right things to champion at the right time.

  At the time, the transformation he was championing was called Salesforce 1, the replatforming of the core applications around social and mobile capabilities. This called for deep sacrifices from the performance zone, which had to forego a whole raft of promised features in order to get this effort over the finish line. But this is where the company showed its best colors. The entire executive team was aligned in supporting the effort. Frankly, I had never seen anything like it.

What Changed

A lot changed in a very short amount of time, but interestingly, I was not there to witness it. After I did my presentation, I moved on to other things, and it was not until late in the fall of 2013 that Marc reached out again. He said he thought they were making some good progress on the recommendations I had made and that it would be valuable for me to come in and do a reality check. So I pulled out the prior work and went off to interview a list of twenty-seven executives, many for the second time. Almost a year to the day, I gave my readout to the team at another executive offsite. Here is what I had learned, again seen through the lenses of the zones:

- *Performance Zone.* Just days after my first presentation Keith Block had joined Salesforce as president and vice-chairman, heading up all customer-facing operations. Basically, he, along with Alex Dayon, head of products, led the installation of a much better-structured performance matrix. Today Salesforce has unique row owners for each of its four material lines of business—Sales Cloud, Service Cloud, Marketing Cloud, and Platform— and unique column owners for its material sources of revenue, organized around three global theaters and two major sales channels, Commercial and Enterprise. The row owners are empowered as GMs, the column owners as theater leads, and both report out at the quarterly business reviews, and there is no question as to their authority in driving results for their row or column.

In addition there are two currently subscale rows in the performance matrix for Communities and Analytics and two subscale theaters in Asia Pacific and Japan. For all of my emphasis on no subscale entities in the matrix, this has proven to be a manageable mix, showing that imperfect adherence to the 10 percent model is not a showstopper, provided it is done in moderation. Subscale rows and columns compete for attention with variable results, but there is a collaborative spirit in the culture that is biased to offer the helping hand provided the effort is on the right track.

Cell-level accountability, on the other hand, is still weak; subtotals garner the bulk of the attention, and how those numbers are achieved is less of a concern. This works all right in high-growth categories where new segments often light up at unpredictable times and getting overly specific could actually bog you down. But as categories mature—and this applies to Sales Cloud and Service Cloud in particular—it is becoming more and more important to enforce the cell-level accountability discipline.

- *Productivity Zone.* Again, newly hired executives have helped change the landscape dramatically. Lynn Vojvodich took the reins in marketing, and her team helped put in place a system for lead generation that hums. Randy Kerns came in from running data centers for Microsoft Azure and is leading the standardization of the same for Salesforce. Mark Hawkins has come over from Autodesk as CFO and teamed up with Burke Norton, who joined from Expedia, to run the general and administrative functions, again with a focus on systems.

The point of these and other changes is that *systems* are beginning to get their due attention at Salesforce. This has not led to any lack of enthusiasm for programs, just an acknowledgment that each has its place, and neither substitutes for the other.

In seeking the right balance between programs and systems, two factors play a big role—business model and rate of growth. Lines of business competing in mature categories with a B2C volume operations business model are best served by leaning more toward systems; by contrast, companies competing in emerging categories with a B2B complex systems business model are best served by leaning more toward programs. Programs apply a burst of energy at a particular point in time to change the inertial momentum of a target process or practice. It is much easier for programs than systems to adapt both to the frequent changes of emerging categories and to the specific demands of very important customers. And that describes Salesforce very well.

- *Incubation Zone.* Here the changes have been remarkable indeed. Marc embraced the notion that when it becomes clear that an incubation effort is not going to scale on its own to become a new row in the performance matrix, it can still make a material contribution by integrating with an existing line of business there. In this context, Data.com became connected to the Sales Cloud, as did Pardot, which was a company ExactTarget acquired prior to the Salesforce acquisition. Desk.com, bought to compete at the low end of the service market, was brought into alignment with the Service Cloud. BuddyMedia and Radian6 were connected into ExactTarget to form the Social Studio in the Marketing Cloud. Other ventures were simply shut down. The result has been to create new space in the zone for Communities and Analytics, followed by the acquisition of RelateIQ. These are all still incubational in the sense that they could become independent rows in the performance matrix or take one of the other exit paths. That is for the future to decide.

- *Transformation Zone.* The big change here was pulling Marketing Cloud into the transformation zone and driving it to scale. By consolidating the assets of three acquisitions, Marc had created enough mass for scale, but would the parts stick together to make a coherent row in the performance matrix, and would the sales team be able to absorb this new set of customers and offers? While it is still a work in progress, the answer appears to be yes.

On the row side, the challenge for GM Scott McCorkle is to creatively apply the four zones model inside his Marketing Cloud while fulfilling its external commitments to the performance zone. To do so, he must integrate and optimize social media assets that were developed on independent architectures (productivity zone), leverage his core email marketing business that is still riding a wave of secular growth (performance zone), continue to nurture and grow JourneyBuilder, a crown jewel that unlocks the power of automated marketing (incubation zone), and bring it to scale as rapidly as possible (transformation zone), all while still meeting his performance zone commitments to Salesforce at large.

On the column side, the challenge is for Keith Block and his team to expand sales capacity beyond the original ExactTarget sales force to leverage the full power of the performance matrix. This means taking on a new target customer, the CMO in a B2C company, a new set of use cases more tuned more to volume operations than complex systems, and a new basis for value creation focused more on campaign effectiveness than on organizational efficiency. The good news is the customer budget is already there; the challenge is for the new arrivals to go get it.

Looking back over this period, the most striking thing was the speed and depth of the changes Marc and his team implemented in just one year. Yes, the four zones framework was a catalyst, but there were at least three other powerful forces at work, ones we should take note of and learn from.

The first is Salesforce's V2MOM management system, the acronym standing for *Vision, Values, Methods, Obstacles, and Metrics.* This system was installed by Marc and his cofounder Parker Harris at the company's inception, and it has been the backbone of its execution success from the start. At its core is the discipline of *methods*, in which each leader distills what he or she will commit to making sure gets done in the coming year. This starts with Marc. His V2MOM sets the table for the whole company. His direct reports then chain their V2MOMs off of his, taking some portion of what he promised to see get done and making that their promise. Then their direct reports do the same, and so on, all the way down, such that everyone at Salesforce publishes his or her own V2MOM and all chain all the way back up to the CEO's.

What further strengthens this approach is that each person's list of methods is presented in priority order, the prioritization being established after vigorous dialog with their peers and their bosses. Again, this starts at the top, with Marc socializing an early draft of his V2MOM for input and criticism. Once its methods are clarified and prioritized, then everyone else's prioritization chains off of it. This prioritization works in large part because the process is open, authentic, and humble (not in its aspirations but in everyone's willingness to serve). The resulting alignment is extraordinary.

The second of Salesforce's core strengths is generosity of spirit. This is manifest in many things the company does but nowhere more so than in its 1-1-1 integrated philanthropy system for giving back. Under this system Salesforce as a company has given 1 percent of its equity and every year gives 1 percent of its product and 1 percent of its employees' time to charitable causes. By building generosity into its core structure the company is redefining the role of the corporation in philanthropy, but just as important, it is attracting and retaining people who genuinely care and want to serve. That spirit spills over into everything they do and gets amplified many times over by events like Dreamforce, where it can inspire tens of thousands of people to lean in all at the same time. This is why the company can punch so far above its weight class. In a tech landscape anchored by far larger enterprises, it is Salesforce who leads. They are the company all of enterprise computing is looking to for guidance and direction.

Finally, from the combination of disciplined execution and generosity of spirit arises the company's third great strength, a culture that marries collaboration to competitiveness. The former helps remove roadblocks to success—V2MOM's *obstacles*—while the latter enforces strict accountability for results—V2MOM's *metrics*. The result is business played as a team sport, the very thing that has brought world championships in both baseball and basketball to the Bay Area of late. This sort of performance is all about tone at the top. If the leadership truly exemplifies these values, the rest of the organization will too. And here I would be remiss if I did not give a shout-out to Parker Harris, Marc's cofounder and head of product strategy and service delivery. I have never met anyone who embodies this synthesis of collaboration and competition better than he does, and it has been an honor to work with him and his team.

At the end of the day, while I am proud that zone management frameworks are making a contribution to the company's current success, in actuality they are only vocabulary. Yes, they help sharpen the focus on what needs to get done and how, but they do not substitute for actually doing it. They do not substitute for team.

Playing Zone Defense:
The Example of Microsoft

As challenging as it is to play zone offense, it is even more challenging to play zone defense. You still have all the challenges of managing across three horizons, and you still have to work through the nasty dynamics of Horizon 2, but in addition you have just taken a hit to your core business in Horizon 1. This is deeply destabilizing to all four zones of management, and you must act swiftly to rectify the situation. At the same time, regaining your footing is no more than an urgent first step on a longer journey to reclaim your identity. In the tech sector at present no company is more directly under attack than Microsoft. It is a testimony to its current leadership, as well as to its heritage, that it is rising to the occasion so well.

I was first introduced to the current team at Microsoft through a meeting with Qi Lu, back in 2012 when he was head of the Online Services Division, which had responsibility for its online property MSN and its newly launched search engine Bing. I got to work with his team shortly thereafter as he pioneered the application of the four zones model inside his own organization. Through Qi, I met Satya Nadella, then president of the Server and Tools Division, the group that was shepherding cloud computing into the Microsoft portfolio via the Azure offer set. Subsequently, these two men have risen in prominence dramatically, Satya as the new CEO, Qi as the executive vice-president of the Applications and Services Group (ASG), a group that includes all of the Office products and services and is responsible for close to a third of the company's revenues, and the majority of its profit.

Both men exemplify a style of leadership that is new to Microsoft. As much as the prior regime was characterized by proud, relentless competitiveness, this new one is marked by a spirit of humility and open collaboration. Everything they say and do communicates a new tone, one that is much more focused on finding new ways for Microsoft to serve its customers than on putting down its competitors, one that values partners as strategic allies rather than tactical stepping-stones. This is a much-needed breath of fresh air as Microsoft's imperial legacy has left a lot of bad feelings in its wake. Transformations cannot be accomplished without others helping voluntarily, and people don't help unless you engage and enlist them first. The new team is showing it has this gift.

With that in mind, let us look at the hand they were dealt through the lenses of the four zones and then see how they are going about playing it.

The Trouble Microsoft Finds Itself In

- *Performance Zone.* Microsoft's performance matrix has traditionally been driven by three core business engines—the Windows operating system, the Office suite of end-user applications, and the server suite of back office applications and systems software. Each has sustained a direct hit in the first decade of this century:
  - *Windows* has been disrupted by the rise of smartphones led by Apple and Google, driving the proliferation of two new on-device operating systems, iOS and Android. Together,

they dominate the landscape of mobile computing to the virtual exclusion of Windows. Moreover, because smartphones and tablets are now broadly adopted in both consumer and business contexts and continuing to proliferate at a rapid rate, they have become the number-one target platform for software developers, thus taking even more attention away from Windows. For the first time in its history, Windows can no longer claim to be the default operating system for end-user computing in client-server applications, something that has profound implications for enterprise IT and represents a huge fall from grace.

- *Office* has come under direct attack by Google Apps and on two fronts. In the consumer space Google gives away its competing software for free, monetizing it directly through advertising and indirectly through data mining. On the enterprise front, Google Apps has flanked Office's stronghold in *personal computing* with a thrust into *collaborative computing*. That is, instead of focusing on individuals producing documents to be presented in finished form, it has focused on teams developing plans, designs, and intellectual property that are continually evolving. This aligns them with the rise of a collaborative work style that is spreading throughout the tech sector and beyond. In particular, collaborative computing is especially well suited to both education and small business applications, two areas where Google Apps is making strong inroads, thereby eroding Office's position with the next generation.

- *On-premise servers* have been a workhorse row in the performance matrix for a very long time, anchoring Microsoft's position in enterprise computing. Here the company has been targeted by Amazon with its web services approach to cloud computing. This has revolutionized the entire IT sector, bringing in a whole new business model (subscription services displacing licensed products), a whole new operating model (self service displacing installation and maintenance), and a whole new infrastructure model (automated computer farms displacing uniquely configured computer clusters). The whole world of on-premise computing has been stood on its ear, and growth here is as challenged as it is in the company's other two lines of business.

Suffice it to say, the rows in the performance matrix have their hands full, but so too do the columns. The OEM sales channel for Windows, long the pacesetter for all things Microsoft, has fallen onto hard times as growth migrates away from the PC to smartphones and tablets. With Dell taking itself private and HP spinning off its PC and printer businesses, neither can be expected to be engines of growth anytime soon. Office is less challenged in the short term, but it needs a freemium go-to-market motion to compete with Google, something that is wholly new to the Microsoft playbook. And cloud computing, where Microsoft Azure has to its credit already made a strong play, requires the company to reengineer a whole raft of enterprise license agreements. In the meantime, the strategy that every three years new versions of Windows and Office would drive worldwide upgrades, the flywheel that has driven Microsoft returns for two decades, has proven less and less viable. In sum, all the company's best go-to plays have run out of steam, and it is not obvious what is going to replace them.

- *Productivity Zone.* Microsoft has been one of the most productive companies on the planet for decades. Having established its effectiveness long ago, it has over the years honed its efficiency by converting more and more programs to systems. This has allowed the company to generate hoards of cash, allowing it to dividend billions back to shareholders. All this was goodness until disruptions hit the core business. Now the company needs to use programs to reengineer its systems in order to free its future from the pull of the past, and frankly, its program muscles have grown a bit weak from atrophy.

  Specifically, here are some of the challenges it must embrace in the productivity zone:
  - Migrate its consumer marketing from brand advertising, imposed from the outside in, to viral engagement emerging inside out organically from the user experience.
  - Migrate its enterprise marketing from high-volume horizontal use cases driving tiered

pricing bundles to high-value vertical use cases driving usage-based pricing based on consumption.

- Reengineer its software release cadence from a product-centric three-year cycle to a service-centric six-month cycle.
- Apply the Six Levers to both its engineering and its sales organizations to unlock talent frozen in place by legacy systems and out-of-data entitlements.
- Realign its offshore development capabilities in China and India from a task-based outsourcing model to an offer-based development model, both to leverage global talent and to open up two high-potential emerging markets.
- Revitalize its developer ecosystem, once the envy of the entire industry, now fallen into disrepair.

When you consider the sheer size of these organizations and the amount of inertia that must be overcome to achieve these ends, the challenges of the productivity zone are daunting indeed.

• *Incubation Zone.* Microsoft has never been much of an incubator. Its classic market triumphs are based on a fast-follower strategy that overtakes an early market leader. In the 1990s Windows took over the GUI market from Macintosh, NT the local area network market from Novell, Word the word-processing market from WordPerfect, Excel the spreadsheet market from Lotus, and Internet Explorer the browser market from Netscape. However, as the company continued to grow in scale, it became harder and harder for any new line of business to even aspire to the size needed to compete against the big guns for resources in the performance matrix. Even the success of xBox, a multibillion-dollar franchise, does not really move the needle in a company the size of Microsoft.

We've seen this before with hypersuccessful franchises. It happened to Xerox, which was never able to profit from its amazing R&D engine at the Palo Alto Research Center. Ditto for Kodak, which actually invented digital photography. Ditto for Intel, where its flagship product, the x86 microprocessor, was once dubbed a creosote bush by its CEO because nothing could grow underneath it. What happens in cases such as these is that R&D becomes increasingly futuristic and fanciful, just to give itself some breathing room, but in so doing it loses all claim to any Horizon 2 commitment in the near-to-medium term. And when it does come time to test fly any of these options, the crucial foundational elements of the Independent Operating Unit with an entrepreneurial GM are glaringly absent.

As a consequence of these dynamics, when Microsoft came under attack in the past decade, it looked to outside acquisitions to help mount a counterattack. Thus it acquired aQuantive to fight Google in the digital advertising space and Nokia to fight Apple and Google in the mobile device arena. Both of these acquisitions came up short and resulted in painful write-downs. You just can't bolt an external entity onto an existing performance matrix without there being an inside entity to help hold it in place. M&A can scale organic incubation, but it cannot substitute for it. Microsoft found itself way out of position.

- *Transformation Zone.* Like many of the tech sector giants that rose to global dominance in the dot-com era, Microsoft has not led a successful transformation zone initiative in this century. Neither has IBM, Cisco, HP, Dell, or Intel. They didn't need to. Well, now they do. Here's what their CEOs are up against:
  - Deeply entrenched legacy franchises that are unable or unwilling to embrace the new realities and make the sacrifices necessary to adapt.
  - Sullen customer bases resentful of the high maintenance fees that have been extracted from them because they had no viable alternative but to pay up.
  - Tired partner ecosystems that have been bled to the bone by draconian price negotiations and are now fighting over the scraps in a market with lackluster growth.
  - Unsympathetic investors who demand continually improving performance from an increasingly decaying base.
  - An internal culture that is rife with entitlement, politics, and cynicism, and has seen many of its best players leave.

These are the kinds of things that brought down the fifty-six companies cited in our first chapter. This is why playing defense is so much harder than playing offense. It just seems obvious that there is no way to win.

So if that is the case, how can Microsoft be so optimistic about its future?

Microsoft Knows How to Play Defense

Recall the principles of using the transformation zone to play defense. The CEO galvanizes the entire company around a three-point plan: *Neutralize first, optimize second, differentiate third.* Galvanizing, however, requires a new burst of energy, and for that Microsoft needed a new leadership style. Satya and his team are supplying that. Let's see how they are making use of it.

- *Neutralize first.* Right from the outset Satya declared Microsoft's top two priorities unequivocally: *Mobile first, Cloud first!* This is exactly the kind of *neutralize first* response that zone defense requires. To paraphrase Marshal Foch, the World War I general, "Apple and Google are crushing my center in mobile while Amazon and Google are driving me back in the cloud—situation excellent, I am attacking!"

  On the cloud front, Microsoft has already made considerable headway with its Azure set of offerings, an effort that Satya himself led when he was heading up that side of the business and is now headed up by his then-lieutenant, Scott Guthrie. While both Amazon and Google have a big head start, both are essentially consumer-first, developer-oriented franchises, and this gives Microsoft a big opening. Most enterprise CIOs, the ones who will be directing a huge amount of cloud computing expenditures in the coming decade, would much prefer to work with a more enterprise-oriented provider that they already know, one that is familiar with the complexities of their systems and their regulatory and security concerns. There are still plenty of battles to be fought, but Microsoft has put itself in a good position to win them.

On the mobile front, by contrast, the landscape is more daunting. There is no realistic prospect of taking material market share at the device level any time soon. That means Microsoft's classic go-to play of leading with Windows and following with Office is not viable here. So instead the *mobile first, cloud first* strategy is being spearheaded by the Office side of the house with ASG delivering a one-two punch. This is the effort being headed by Qi Lu.

On the mobile side, coincident with Satya being appointed CEO, ASG released Office on both iOS and Android, making it available for download from the Apple and Google app stores free of charge. This is allowing Microsoft to keep connection with professionals who use Office on their desktop but need access to it on their mobile devices. And on the cloud side, Qi has made ASG's number-one priority migrating as much of the customer base as possible as fast as possible to Office 365, Microsoft's cloud-based version of the Office suite. This is aligning well with the priorities of enterprise CIOs, most of whom are under pressure to reduce their support costs, in part by getting out of the desktop maintenance business as much as they can. One of the beauties of cloud computing is that you update once centrally and deploy everywhere else basically instantaneously.

Finally, Qi and his team have targeted a third threat to neutralize, this one specific to ASG itself, focused on blunting the challenge directed squarely at Office by Google Apps. As noted, Google's approach to knowledge worker productivity has been to relocate the productivity focus on collaboration. This reflects fundamental changes under way both in the structure of work and in the culture of the workforce. Personal computing products like Word, Excel, and PowerPoint still get a ton of work done, but now they need to be supplemented with new communications and messaging platforms like Skype, new file-sharing options like OneDrive, new content creation applications like Sway, new content discovery engines like Delve, and new user interaction modalities like OneNote, all of which have been prioritized under the new regime, even though the anchor products are still the prime revenue generators.

What has allowed the new leadership team to make such rapid progress on the *neutralize first* front is their willingness to confront a challenging reality forcefully yet humbly. Their messaging is clear. *We are behind. This is what we must do to catch up. This is what our customers want us to do. Let's just get it done. And let us also understand there is a price to pay.* When you invest in your future power, your present performance takes a hit. Market share in the near term will likely go down. So too will gross margins. Microsoft no longer enjoys the position of dominance it once did. Its investors understand this and will support the new directions up to a point, but only so far. That is why optimization is the second part of the zone defense playbook.

*   *Optimize second.* This is the weakest link in Microsoft's defense. Its imperial heritage has never required it to optimize in the past, that role being passed on to its OEMs while it continued to extract premium rents. Moreover, its longtime emphasis on achieving productivity through systems has created a legacy that is hard to modify at a time when flexibility and agility are required. Perhaps most importantly, its culture has always been about fierce competition for resources, the goal always being to keep whatever you have and get as much more as you can.

In the near term, therefore, optimization is primarily taking the form of downsizing and divestiture. The company has announced that it will be making a series of tough choices, all aimed at focusing the company more directly on its mission to deliver productivity, first at work, then extending to the home. It has attractive properties to sell, and this capital can be used to fund work streams targeting high-growth market opportunities. And that is a beginning.

But much of what Microsoft is getting done today is being achieved by following its old ways, and that is not sustainable. The company must learn how to extract resources from context to repurpose for core. It must learn how to field programs that amplify its effectiveness in new development and go-to-market motions. And with its legacy systems, it must learn to use Six Sigma and the Six Levers creatively, not as techniques for grudgingly capitulating to changes it cannot compete with, but rather for creating fitness to meet those new challenges. The road ahead is clear—it just needs to have more cars on it.

- *Differentiate third.* In contrast to its challenges with optimization, Microsoft's prospects for incubation have never been greater. In ASG, in particular, they are legion. Begin with Bing. Its core job is to be a search engine that competes with Google, and through rigorous neutralization and optimization it has achieved a profitable sustainable business in so doing. Beyond that, however, Bing is now embedded in Windows, giving the latter not only device-based but also enterprise-based search capabilities as well as giving it a mechanism for monetizing freemium offers. And most importantly, Bing's daily logs of millions of queries and answers provides a rich feed for Microsoft's machine learning engines. These engines in turn are developing maps and algorithms to better understand and predict, well, anything— from a graph of work that shows where the nodes of knowledge are and who are their critical contributors to a graph of the world that can enable smarter roads, smarter buildings, smarter cities, and—dare we say—a smarter planet.

And that is just Bing. There are also Sway and Planner and Delve and Lockbox and Skype and Cortana. What makes these nascent offers much more strategic than their predecessors is that they are organically connected to the mobile first, cloud first mission. Their first-generation instances fit right into the performance matrix. At the same time, however, the underlying platform of machine learning upon which they are based is itself a disruptive innovation that will fundamentally change the basis of productivity software across the sector. By building this fabric into Office itself, by making it available across device platforms and open to both customer and third-party developers, Microsoft can redefine the landscape of end-user computing once again. It is a very heady time indeed.

Concluding Remarks

It is time to bring this book to a close. Let's recap the journey we have been on. In chapter one we surveyed the impact of disruptive innovation on established enterprises and called attention to the crisis of prioritization it triggers. In chapter two we described a management system we called *zone management*, one specifically designed to cope with this crisis. It is built around four zones—the performance zone, the productivity zone, the incubation zone, and the transformation zone—each with unique methods, obstacles, and metrics. The essence of the model is that each of these zones must be managed separately from the other three, and to that end, chapters three through six described the approaches needed by each zone. In chapter seven we distilled all this down to an installation procedure that aligns zone management with the annual planning process, and in this final chapter we have looked at Salesforce and Microsoft as two case examples of these models in action.

So where might you go from here? Basically, what you have is a set of frameworks. They are intended to describe the state of enterprises operating in business categories that are being fundamentally disrupted. The question is: is your business one of them, and if so, do these models indeed shed light on your current situation? If the answer is yes, then at minimum you want to engage your management team with this vocabulary in order to have a common language for dealing with the raft of changes coming your way. If that vocabulary resonates, then a follow-on step would be to commit to applying these frameworks to creating your next annual plan, following the outline in chapter seven, and to use them in the following year during quarterly business reviews to track your progress. For any given company, that involves more variables than this author can envision. All I can say by way of farewell is that I have done my best to provide a vehicle for the journey, and I wish you the very best of outcomes should you choose to undertake it.

Acknowledgments

The material for this book came out of a series of client engagements that had a big impact on my thinking. The two most prominent were featured in the final chapter, and I would be remiss in not thanking Marc Benioff and Qi Lu once again for sponsoring these efforts. In addition, I learned a lot from working with Mike DeCesare and the McAfee team at Intel; Dominic Orr, Keerti Melkote, and the executive team at Aruba (now part of HP); Steve Smith, Charles Meyers, and the team at Equinix; Lip-Bu Tan, Qi Wang, and the team at Cadence; Gary Kovacs and the team at AVG; Keith Krach and the team at Docusign; and George Oliver, Robert Locke, and the team at Tyco. Whenever frameworks engage with real-world challenges, they come away modified in some way and very much the better for it. Thanks to all involved for your creative engagement and your patience.

In addition, as part of the writing process this time around, I posted early drafts for each of the chapters in this book on my LinkedIn Influencers blog. I got numerous valuable comments from a host of people, many of which had a significant impact on the final draft. In that context I would like to acknowledge the following: Jonathan Dippert, Mike Frazzini, Don Sheppard, Anna Sidana, Patti Dock, Nicole France, Richard Jaenicke, Stephen Wood, George Gilbert, Rahul Abhyankar, Alistair Sim, Martin Carroll, Dennis O'Flynn, Les Trachtman, Somesh Bhagat, Dean Hager, Steven Webster, Robert Joynson, William Malek, Suresh Nirody, Fred Orensky, David Rader, Joel Polanco, Chris Schreiner, Ronny Max, Paul Hobcraft, John Steinert, Jan Dornbach, David Swan, Bud Michael, Hank Barnes, Ron Askeland, and John Morris. It is a wonderful thing for an author to engage with readers prior to final publication, and I very much appreciated doing so in this context.

Finally, with this book as with every other, I simply could not write at all without the extraordinary support I am so lucky to have. At the publishing end, once again I have relied on my longtime friend and agent Jim Levine, ably helped by his colleague Kerry Sparks, at the Levine Greenberg Rostan Literary Agency, who in turn put me in touch with Mary Cummings and her team at Diversion: a big shout out and thanks to all. At work, support begins with the partnership at Mohr Davidow where as a venture partner I hang my shingle. The general partners and administrative team there graciously support my errant and itinerant ways. Closer to home, Pat Granger manages all my "context" obligations far better than I ever could, allowing me to have time to focus on my "core." She is simply the best, and she is ably assisted by a cohort made up of Nanette Vidan-Peled, Roth Hensley, Jonathan Dippert, Donel Bozajeski, Rich Stimbra, and Kim

Atkins, and I want to thank them all for making my work life work as well as it does.

At home there is Marie—first, last, and always. We are nearing a very special anniversary made even more so by our daughter Margaret and her husband Daniel, our son Michael, our daughter Anna and her husband Dave, and the newest member of the family, our first grandchild, Noah. Family is what makes it all worthwhile, and Marie has led ours from the very beginning. It is a wonderful feeling to be her devoted husband.

Index

Note: page numbers in *italics* indicate figures or tables.

CPSIA information can be obtained at www.ICGtesting.com
Printed in the USA
BVOW11*2206031115

425103BV00005B/8/P